AN EDUCATOR'S GUIDE TO USING YOUR
3 EYES

*How to Apply Intellect, Insight, and Intuition to
Promote Personal and School-Wide Transformation*

MEGAN R. SWEET, ED.D.

BALBOA.
PRESS
A DIVISION OF HAY HOUSE

Balboa Press books may be ordered through booksellers or by contacting:

Balboa Press
A Division of Hay House
1663 Liberty Drive
Bloomington, IN 47403
www.balboapress.com
1 (877) 407-4847

Print information available on the last page.

ISBN: 978-1-9822-1527-9 (sc)
ISBN: 978-1-9822-1526-2 (hc)
ISBN: 978-1-9822-1525-5 (e)

Library of Congress Control Number: 2018912935

Balboa Press rev. date: 11/14/2018

For my son Malcolm.

Contents

Preface

Curiosity Invites Connection

> I vow to be curious.
> to start conversations.
> to listen with intention.
> to stay open.
> to inquire.
> to be willing to be
> surprised by what I don't
> yet know about another.
> to let this be my practice. (Boelman, 2017)

Curiosity is open, reflective, and expansive. It doesn't have fixed answers. It wants to know more; it wants to grow and improve. Curiosity also lacks judgment or blame. Curiosity allows us to explore what isn't working without being harsh on the people and circumstances that created it. Curiosity is born of love.

This is my invitation as you read the book. To be curious. To be curious about yourself, including your thoughts and beliefs. To be curious about your students, who they are, how they learn, and how you respond to them. To be curious about your peers, what's important to them, what makes them tick.

Curiosity is essential for the journey ahead because this book offers a new way of seeing yourself and of approaching our education system. I invite your curiosity to consider what is included here, to allow it to push your thinking or confirm your deepest beliefs. I encourage you to suspend any reflexive doubt that can come as we contemplate new ideas. Instead, I invite you to lean into the expansiveness of possibility.

We will use three lenses (the 3 Eyes) to support this new way of seeing: Intellect, Insight, and Intuition. Each lens provides us with a unique way to understand and interpret the world. Used together, they facilitate a depth of perception that makes our challenges and their solutions easier to see. Curiosity expands our ability to see in this new way.

What do you get for being curious? An opportunity to develop a deeper and more heart-centered relationship with yourself. To learn to love and appreciate yourself more while you simultaneously work on the persistent beliefs and patterns that undermine your potential. To develop a new and more balanced way of experiencing your life that comes with a new and more empowered way to move through it. In the book, this is called doing self-work.

You will also learn new ways to approach our education system. As we strive to prepare all students for college, career, and community, the stakes are high, and the stressors can seem never-ending. It can feel like we are swimming upstream; buffeted by budget constraints, systemic inequities, and insufficient professional support. Rather than continuing to struggle against the currents of a system that isn't working, I believe that is it time that we change course. I ask that you lean into your curiosity to consider the premise that the best way to transform our education system is from the inside-out by using its greatest assets—the people.

At its roots, education is a social enterprise; it must be done in community rather than in isolation. As such, the solution to improving our education system comes from building on the strengths of that community. This book explores the potential transformation that could happen to the whole system if we put more time and attention into developing our educators. It asserts that if we provide our teachers and leaders with strategies to understand themselves better through *self-work*, they will be better able to create supportive places for all students to learn and grow through *school-work*.

This school-work leverages the power of the whole to support the self-actualization of the parts. To create the educational system of the 21ˢᵗ century, we must support educators to do self-work alongside school-work.

Throughout this book, we will explore just why self-work and school-work form a powerful combination. We will learn why coming to love and accept oneself is the first step towards creating an educational system that serves all students. Through the 3 Eyes, we will learn how to see ourselves, our peers, and our students with more clarity. Through practices grounded in love and compassion, we will learn to use the information gleaned from the 3 Eyes to lead to personal and school-wide transformation.

Much of the content here encourages you to approach life with just a bit more trust. You'll be asked to try some new practices, to augment some of your tried and true ways of being, and to let go of what no longer serves you. Curiosity, born of love for self and other, is all that you need to take this journey. So, please join me in developing this more in-depth way of approaching your life and our education system. Be ready to end the journey more grounded, in appreciation of yourself, and more hopeful for the way forward to educate our youth.

Let's Do This!

I'm a work in progress. This fact will become abundantly clear as you read the book. Some of you will be able to relate to the challenges I share and find solace and in my story. Some of you will scratch your heads and wonder why I get tripped up the way that I do. The great thing is that for the first time in my life, I'm okay with my challenges. In fact, I embrace them. That's the real story I am seeking to tell here. While the journey I will describe began with a simple desire to feel better, it has turned into a new way of approaching all aspects of my life. It also has changed how I understand the challenges in our education system.

I share the information here, then, as both a humble offering and as a call to action. I offer my experiences as an example that if a hard case like me can experience the benefits that I have from using the 3 Eyes, then I believe that anyone can. This as a call to action because through my lifetime in education, I've yet to see reforms that produce widespread equitable outcomes for students. I've got some ideas about how we can address those inequities. I am asking all of you, as colleagues, to consider these ideas within your context and then do something about it.

Before we get into where I am now and into the contents of this book, it is helpful to understand a bit more about where I've been. I grew up in Berkeley, California, the product of hippy parents and the middle of three girls. My childhood was in the backdrop of the famous free speech movement on the University of California (UC) at Berkeley campus in the 1960's. The energy of that time continued through the culture of protests, community activism, and freedom of expression that permeated my town in the 70's and 80's.

Growing up in Berkeley, kids were encouraged to form their own opinions and question authority, even that of our parents and teachers.

I grew up poor, but in a middle-class neighborhood. To make ends meet, my parents rented a part of our house to foreign exchange students who came to Berkeley to learn English. They joined us for breakfast every morning and used our one telephone when they needed to make calls (in the good old days when phones were stuck to walls, and there wasn't an abundance of them). I spent most of my childhood learning about people from around the world, including Japan, Switzerland, France, Spain, and Brazil. I got to explore many different foods and cultures over the dining room table and became particularly immersed and interested in Japanese traditions. Many of the students became a part of our family, traveling with us and joining us for family celebrations. Many of those students are still close friends to this day.

While at home I was learning about the world, at school, I learned about social justice alongside reading and math. The Equal Rights Amendment (stating that a person's rights could not be denied based on gender) was passed a by Congress few months before I was born in 1972. For it to be added to our Constitution, three-quarters (38) of the states needed to ratify it. By the time I was seven, we were still a few states shy of 38. Rallies across the country called for states to ratify the Equal Rights Amendment (ERA), including at least one I distinctly remember at my elementary school. I can still see myself standing in a large circle on our field, chanting along with my classmates and our parents that girls had rights too. By age 10, the ERA was still three states short and failed to be added to the Constitution. I remember the outrage in my community about this. We are still one state shy of 38 today.

In addition to women's rights, we also discussed equality and racism as a part of many of my classes. One of my elementary schools was named after Malcolm X, a human rights activist and leader in the Civil Rights Movement. We learned about his approach to promoting equality alongside Martin Luther King, Jr. I also learned about the plight of Native Americans, about the Japanese Internment during World War Two, the Holocaust, and so much more. We were taught to be critical thinkers and to ask questions.

Through my classroom experiences, I developed a sense of justice and a commitment to equality.

I also grew up in a time before there were many standards for instruction in school. In elementary school, one of my teachers had us meditate daily while another made us sell chayote (a prickly cactus-like vegetable) for our class fundraiser. I had an excellent 8th grade English and History teacher who inspired my creativity and a 7th-grade science teacher who was downright dangerous, smashing glass beakers at students' feet when he was angry. From my 8th grade teacher, I learned how to love history. From my 7th grade teacher, I learned that adults had limits and I would do well to know where they were.

During my teen years, I cut school with my friends more than I should have. It was equally within the realm of possibility during those moments of freedom to participate in anti-Apartheid protests or goof off and smoke clove cigarettes, both of which happened on the UC Berkeley campus.

I decided I wanted to be a teacher in 6th grade. That year, I had Mr. Harris, who is hands-down the best teacher I ever had. Mr. Harris made school fun and engaging, took a genuine interest in our lives, and shared his life with us. He held us accountable, cried while reading us *Where the Red Fern Grows*, and encouraged us to express ourselves. Being in Mr. Harris' class felt electric. He made learning an adventure, both in the classroom and on the many field trips and activities he planned for us. For example, he took my whole class on a bike ride through Berkeley—as a former teacher, my nerves twinge just thinking about it. As a kid, it was a blast.

Regardless of my inspiration from Mr. Harris, I do remember struggling to find myself as a student, especially in classes that felt chaotic and unstructured. I am not an auditory learner, and therefore I spent a lot of my childhood struggling to connect with what was happening in classes where teacher talk dominated the lessons. My performance as a student was also heavily influenced by whom I had as a teacher and whether they could see the potential behind my smart mouth and inconsistent performance. For example, in second grade, I was in the lowest reading group, but in third grade, I was in the gifted and talented program. I won a writing award in high school, but my counselor told me that I wasn't college material.

Through these experiences, the idea solidified in my mind that I was meant to be a teacher. I knew I could make class feel better for people like me, the kids who did not take to school easily, but who had potential when under the right care. And that's exactly what I did. On the day after I graduated from college, I started my teacher credential program at Stanford University, just a month shy of my 22nd birthday.

I learned many valuable lessons at Stanford. Firstly, teaching is harder than it looks! I taught high school Social Studies during the day while taking classes in the evening. In my teacher preparation classes, we often discussed race and equity in the United States, particularly as they related to our roles as educators. There, I was introduced to the fact that a Culture of Power exists in this country that advantages white people, particularly those that are middle or upper class (Delpit, 1995).

This had a profound impact on me. Despite growing up in an area grounded in social justice and equality, and in a house where I was regularly exposed to people from around the world, it wasn't until my courses at Stanford that I began to understand how being white made me an "insider." I had access to power and opportunities not afforded to others in this country. It was a painful, sobering, and crucial realization to have as I entered teaching. Since that time, it has been a career-long journey to understand how privilege impacts outcomes for students and to learn to see my privilege more clearly.

All told, I taught for ten years, primarily middle school English and Social Studies. I loved connecting with the kids, the collegiality I shared with my fellow teachers, and the creative process of writing lessons. Teaching is a profession that requires your full self, every day. There were times when I wanted to quit and conversely times when I could not imagine doing anything else.

The longer I taught, the more I felt compelled to be a part of bettering our education system on a larger scale. After ten years in the classroom, I decided to go back to graduate school. I got a credential to be an administrator and my Doctoral degree in Educational Leadership. I studied the impact that a financial intervention could have on improving student achievement.

While finishing my research, I served an assistant principal (AP) at one of the lowest-performing elementary schools in my district, a school that was poised to be redesigned. When a school is redesigned, it means that the school is not successfully serving its students and changes to teaching practices, school culture, and/or general systems are required. My school needed help in all three areas.

A brilliant principal led our design team, and we had an active community of parents, district staff, and teachers who helped us to design a new school. Within a couple of years of starting the redesign, we saw significant gains in our students' academic performance, and within five years, our school became one of the highest-performing elementary schools in the district. My time as an AP was a profound experience, perhaps most significant in demonstrating that change was possible and that it happens in the hands of the people closest to the work—students, parents, teachers, and site administrators.

Since my time as an AP, I have worked both within and outside my school district, leading school-level, district-level, and state-level changes. These changes have included redesigning more schools, implementing district-level reforms, and streamlining processes across district systems. This work has brought me to large urban districts that served tens of thousands of students as well as to small, rural districts that served a small number of students spread across a broad geographic area. Traveling across the state has helped me to appreciate how diverse California is, and how difficult it is to create a one-size-fits-all standard for excellence. Nuance matters when it comes to understanding the needs of students and families and in evaluating the success of the schools that serve them.

With now over 20 years in education under my belt, I will admit that I am concerned. Despite facilitating successful reform initiatives, I have seen that sustaining and building on areas of success can be difficult. Changes to leadership, teacher turnover, and economic constraints make it hard to keep the momentum going. Additionally, I believe that widespread education reforms fail because we have been using an incomplete set of tools. While addressing the external symptoms of student achievement (such as content standards) is essential, student access to high-quality learning experiences remains heavily influenced by race and socioeconomic status.

I have come to believe that unless we address the way that educators understand themselves and their students, then even our most innovative reforms will fail to have a widespread impact. This is true because our minds are incredibly powerful machines that often go unchecked while we go about the business of educating our kids. While we are busy implementing a new curriculum, for example, in the background our minds are providing impressions about ourselves and our abilities, and our students and their abilities, that will either support or hinder that curriculum's success. How?

The answer brings us to the impetus for this book, my self-development journey. Not too long ago, I experienced three successive years of professional setbacks that woke me up—big time. Through those experiences, I came to understand that I was doing some very damaging self-talk that was having an impact on my health and my professional success. That self-talk was the result of negative beliefs I had about myself, beliefs that I didn't realize were there but were nonetheless impacting how I experienced my life.

Through my efforts to understand those beliefs more deeply, I learned that each of us has subconscious and conscious minds that influence the way we show up and interpret our experiences. As I became more familiar with my subconscious and conscious minds, I began to detect how they impacted my self-esteem and my experiences at work and home. I also learned that I could change the thoughts and beliefs that were keeping me from enjoying my life more fully. I dove into making those changes.

Pretty quickly into this self-work, I saw a connection to the broader world of education. I thought of my career where I have worked primarily with communities that do not share my background and of my evolving understanding of race, culture, and privilege over that time. I thought of the instances I have witnessed other educators' limiting beliefs about their efficacy inhibit their success leading classrooms, schools, and districts. I thought about young white teachers in particular and how their (perhaps) unexamined biases were alienating and harming the very students they came to serve, just as they did for me. And, I thought about our students, whose sense of self is shaped by the adults they encounter. They deserve the best possible start in life, which means that they need educators who are self-aware and mindful of the messages they are sending to their students.

So, I did something about it! I combined my two loves; personal development and system redesign, into a process that supports educators to work on themselves while also working on their educational context. Through my own experience, I know that personal development is important and yet it often takes a backseat to the urgent needs we see in our classrooms and schools. What I have discovered, however, is that personal development is crucial to successful school improvement and that both can take place simultaneously. That's what the 3 Eyes framework is all about—clear seeing matched with strategies for the doing.

Goal for This Book

I have come to believe that a key to creating educational settings where children can thrive is through the intentional use of what I refer to as the 3 Eyes: Intellect, Insight, and Intuition. As educators, we're good at the **Intellect** part (higher order thinking skills), that's our job after all! We have been much less practiced, however, with use of **Insight** (understanding how our beliefs, cultural backgrounds, and experiences influence us), and have almost completely ignored our **Intuition** (integrating mindfulness and quiet reflection to access information that exists below our surface thoughts).

Each lens offers one way to see the world, and as such, has its strengths and limitations. Just like the Indian parable about the six blind men and the elephant, when we move through life only using one lens, we are not able to see the whole picture. In the parable, six blind men encounter an elephant and try to discern what it is. Depending on where each blind man is positioned along the elephant, he makes different meaning about what he is facing. The one by the tusk thinks he has encountered a spear, the one by the elephant's side thinks he is facing a wall, the one by its leg thinks he is by a tree, and so on. The parable demonstrates that when we project our partial experience as the whole truth, then we miss vital information that is essential to our complete understanding.

The same is true with the three lenses. Each provides a particular viewpoint, and when used in isolation, fails to give us a complete understanding of our circumstances. Used together, however, we gain a depth of perspective that enables us to see the full elephants in our lives. When we see more clearly, we can make more informed and empowered choices. As a result, we feel more grounded and connected to ourselves, to the people we encounter, and to the world at large.

For us to make a lasting and profound change in education, educators must do *self-work* alongside *school-work* by integrating the information we take in from each of the 3 Eyes to see ourselves, our students and our education system with a new perspective. Self-work starts with educators cultivating a practice of self-care and of addressing the limiting beliefs that thwart their potential. A limiting belief is an idea that holds us back and constrains what we think is possible (about ourselves or others). As educators become more grounded and confident through self-work, then they are better able to engage in school-work. School-work involves addressing the limiting beliefs that influence how educators understand their students and their educational contexts and includes implicit bias. School-work also consists of the doing of school and district reform. My goal for this book, therefore, is to provide information and practical tools for integrating the 3 Eyes (Intellect, Insight, and Intuition) into our educational settings and our personal lives.

Because the 3 Eyes offer us a way to see the world, they also complement other frameworks and strategies. This is intentional. My desire is for people to use the 3 Eyes as a way of experiencing life, and therefore it works to provide greater depth and meaning to every situation. The intended audience for this book is anyone connected to education: teachers, school leaders, district leaders, and school and district staff. For simplicity, I've grouped the various job categories into "educators," but do refer to specific job titles when appropriate. Similarly, I have grouped classrooms, schools, and district offices into "educational settings" but also refer to specific contexts when it makes sense to do so.

If you are reading this, I assume that you believe in kids and want to give them the best possible educational experience. I also assume that you are whole and perfect just as you are, but like all humans, you have personal struggles that can get in your way. My hope is that the concepts in this book will empower you to realize personal transformation as well as to produce improved outcomes for the students you serve.

To sum up, the potential benefits that can be gleaned from this book include:

- Greater self-awareness
- Improved connection with, and appreciation of, oneself
- Understanding of where beliefs come from, how they influence us, and strategies for changing beliefs we do not want
- Improved decision-making
- Improved classroom and school cultures
- Improved student achievement

What This Book is and What it Isn't

This book is...

- A blend of research-based best practices with truths that lie outside of academia.
- Processes and tools for use in educational systems that can and should also be applied towards personal development.

This book is not...

- One-size-fits-all.
- A step-by-step guide or a set of concise tools that can be used without adaptation.

This book is also a combination of meta-analysis and personal reflection. Many of the concepts I share here are not new, and I synthesize others' findings throughout the book. This research serves to create context and meaning for each of the lenses and to provide some baseline information upon which you can begin to build your understanding. In my synthesis of the research, I draw meaning and connections based on my life and experiences. Where appropriate, I also include real-life examples to underscore some of the concepts that I introduce.

Putting the ideas that I share here into the 3 Eyes framework *is* new, especially my premise that self-work and school-work must go hand in hand if we truly want to reform our schools. What is also new is the marriage of ethereal elements (like the intuitive practices we will discuss in this book) with the more traditional structures of our education system. The combination is compelling and has profound implications for our educational system.

Organization of the Book

In the next chapter, we will discuss the foundational principles and the theory of action for using the 3 Eyes framework. Within the subsequent three chapters, we will explain each of the 3 Eyes (Intellect, Insight, and Intuition) in detail, taking care to highlight the big ideas for ease of use. Since this book is about doing self-work alongside school-work, each chapter will conclude with implications for each as well as the story of my relationship with each lens. The final chapter of the book contains a process to apply the 3 Eyes and some thoughts for where to begin.

How to Use this Book

The contents of the book are intended to provoke your thinking. As such, there are sections in each chapter where you are invited to apply the concepts to yourself or your context. They are called, "Make It Yours." Before jumping in, please grab a highlighter, pen, and notebook, or any other means for engaging with the material. Mark things up, ask questions, draw your own conclusions, make this information your own!

Please Note

The names and situations I describe in this book have been changed to protect the privacy of individuals and to maintain the confidentiality I have held in my various roles. Also, in my personal reflection, I am choosing to focus on my professional career, and therefore a lot of my story is left out. This is intentional. Not only do I want to protect the privacy of my friends and family, but also, it was a professional crisis that led me to develop the 3 Eyes. In my narrative, I expand upon how the 3 Eyes led me through that crisis. I am excited to share this information with you!

What's Self-Love Got to Do with It?

"Owning our story and loving ourselves through that process is the bravest thing we'll ever do." Brene Brown

"Training teachers to understand bias will not eliminate it, but it could create an institutional environment in which it is clear that understanding bias and its effects is critically important. The long-term return on investment is inestimable." Soraya Chemaly (2016)

Looking Forward

So, what's self-love got to do with it?? Everything! We've learned that the 3 Eyes framework provides us with a depth of perception that allows us to see ourselves, our lives, and our students with more clarity.

As we'll now discuss in this chapter, coming to greater self-love and compassion is the root of both personal and school-wide transformation. To understand why we will take a 'quick look under the hood' to discuss the interplay between our conscious and subconscious minds and how they influence the way we experience the world around us. In this exploration, we will uncover one of two through lines for the book: learning how to identify and shift limiting thoughts and beliefs that do not align with our conscious desires. This is what is called doing the self-work.

Once we understand more about how our brains work, we will talk about the impact of implicit bias and the inequities of our current education system. In this discussion, we'll uncover the other through-line of the book: supporting educators to create more inclusive settings for students. This is one essential aspect of doing the school-work. Finally, we will introduce the Theory of Action for how the 3 Eyes work together to help us to make more empowered and aligned decisions, to promote improved experiences in our lives, and to create more supportive classrooms for our students. Hint: this is where self-love comes in, big time!

It's time to introduce our first symbol! This stick figure represents us, and they will pop up in every chapter moving forward.

The 3 Eyes: Intellect, Intuition, and Insight

We can define *Intellect, Insight, and Intuition* as follows:

- *Intellect:* Logical thinking and reasoning, comprising those cognitive skills that allow us to compute in math, to analyze problems and to form language.
- *Insight*: Deep understanding of a person or thing (Google, 2017).
- *Intuition*: Knowing something based on instinct or feeling, rather than from conscious reasoning (Google, 2017).

Our intellect is what separates humans from other animals. Not only does it give us the ability to perform complex tasks, but also the self-awareness to observe our thoughts and actions. Intellect is a powerful tool that most of us use without much conscious intention—it is a reflexive practice as natural as breathing.

Through insight, we can understand the interplay of our conscious and subconscious minds and identify the beliefs and cultural norms that influence how we experience the world. Insight also provides us with the ability to learn from our past experiences and to see problems from different points of view. When we use insight, we are better able to make choices that are relevant, timely, and aligned with our current context.

Through intuition, we learn to listen to our inner voice, probing for the underlying thoughts and motivations that are guiding our actions. Accessing our intuition requires slowing down and connecting with our minds and bodies. Intuition is quiet and subtle. An excellent pathway to intuition is mindfulness (being aware of our thoughts and feelings in the present moment).

When we intentionally use our Intellect, Insight, and Intuition together, it is like putting on a pair of 3-Dimensional glasses. Just as 3-D glasses transform a flat, fuzzy image into one that jumps out at us from the page, by looking at our lives, experiences, and decisions through all three lenses, we gain a depth of meaning and level of clarity that we cannot achieve through using one lens alone. When we apply these lenses to our own lives, by doing *self-work*, we become more grounded, confident, and trusting. When we additionally apply these concepts to educational settings, by doing *school-work*, we are better positioned to create spaces where children and adults feel safe and seen, and where real educational transformation can take place.

A Quick Look Under the Hood

An essential part of knowing ourselves better is understanding the interplay between our conscious and subconscious minds and how they influence the way we respond to the world around us. Once armed with that knowledge, we can intentionally use the power of the 3 Eyes to bridge the gap between our conscious thoughts and our subconscious (automatic) responses. This journey of self-discovery requires that we learn a bit about how our brains develop and respond to stimuli. Let's do this!

We are of Two Minds

Understanding how our brains work, and specifically how they respond to our thoughts and emotions, are relatively new fields of scientific study. As such, the definitions for the terms below can vary between experts, and I expect will continue to be refined over time. For this book, we'll use the following meanings:

- **Mind:** The way information that gets transmitted within our bodies, including our thoughts and sensory information (sights, smells, tastes, physical sensations, and sounds)
- **Conscious (mind):** The representation of who we perceive ourselves to be (our hopes, dreams, and individuality); self-awareness (Lipton, 2014)
- **Subconscious (mind):** The warehouse of information that holds our habits, controls our physical responses, and hard-wires learned responses to situations (Lipton, 2014)
- **Unconscious:** The feelings, actions, and reactions that we exhibit, but that we are not always in control of or aware of (such as a knee-jerk response)
- **Programs:** The learned responses to our environment that reside in our subconscious minds and that drive our responses (both conscious and unconscious)

Just as there are several different ways to define these terms, there are several different ways to represent the conscious and subconscious minds. These include icebergs (the conscious mind being the part above the water and subconscious mind the part below) and bullseyes (the conscious mind being the center and the unconscious and subconscious minds being the outer rings).

Dr. Bruce Lipton is a world-renowned scientist who has been on the leading edge of understanding the power of beliefs and how the subconscious and conscious minds work together. Dr. Lipton uses the analogy of a computer to demonstrate the relationship between the two minds. He likens the subconscious mind to a computer's hard drive (ROM), and the conscious mind to the desktop (RAM) (2012). Like the hard drives on our computers, our subconscious minds hold an incredible amount of information, are always online and processing incoming data, and can perform tasks without our conscious awareness or instructions. For example, our subconscious minds keep us breathing and our hearts beating without explicit instructions. They also hold our memories and alert us to danger without prompting. The conscious mind, on the other hand, draws on information stored in the hard drive to make meaning, and contains various features with clear and defined functions, much like programs on a computer. For example, our conscious minds draw on stored memories to make meaning of strange sound or to make connections between two different concepts. We'll discuss the roles of both minds in more detail below.

I like this analogy because it provides a way to understand the discrete roles that each mind performs as well as the give and take of information between the two. We are going to use this analogy throughout the remainder of the book, and the notion of "programming" to refer to the way that our brains take in, store, and respond to information.

Just how powerful and influential are our subconscious minds? While the numbers vary, a general estimate is that they are more than a million times more powerful than our conscious minds. This means that our subconscious minds actively filter upwards of 40 million of bits of information per second as compared to the 40 bits per second that our conscious minds process. Lipton estimates that 95% of the time, our subconscious minds are the ones in control (Lipton, 2012). This is profound because while we identify with our conscious minds and see them as representing who we are, in actuality, our perceptions and responses are heavily influenced by subconscious programs that we may not even be aware of. Oh boy.

Note: If you'd like to know more about the inner workings of our computers and how information is processed in our bodies, check out the *Brain Primer* in the Appendix.

Big Idea #1:

We have both subconscious and conscious minds that work together to shape our experiences and sense of self. Most of the time, it is our subconscious minds that are in control, reacting to stimuli based on past programming.

Two Minds Really Are Better Than One

What are some of the functions of our *computers* and how do the two minds work together? Psychologist and Nobel Prize winner in Economic Science, Dr. Daniel Kahneman, explores the interplay between what I refer to as the subconscious and conscious minds in his book, *Thinking Fast and Slow*. Kahneman (2011) asserts that throughout the day, our brains vacillate between two modes of thinking, which he dubs System 1 (our subconscious minds) and System 2 (our conscious minds). Table one compares the skills, qualities, and challenges of each System.

Table 1: System 1 and System 2 Functions

System 1 (Subconscious) Skills:	System 2 (Conscious) Skills:
• Perceiving the world around us, recognizing objects, orienting attention and avoiding danger • Detecting hostility in a voice • Answering 2+2=? • Understanding simple sentences • Driving a car on an empty road • Completing the phrase, "bread and…"	• Focusing on the voice of a particular person in a crowded and noisy room • Searching memory to identify a surprising sound • Maintaining a faster walking speed than is natural • Filling out a tax form • Telling someone your phone number

System 1 (Subconscious) Qualities:	System 2 (Conscious) Qualities:
• Runs automatically and quickly • Provides information and controls functions involuntarily • Learns through repetition	• Comes into play when System 1 functions cannot address the task or issue at hand • Controls our behavior and suppresses or modifies some impulses from System 1 • Draws on the information held in System 1 to complete more complex tasks
System 1 (Subconscious) Challenges:	System 2 (Conscious) Challenges:
• Cannot be turned off—runs all the time • Has biases and systematic errors that can make mistakes	• Easily distracted—cannot perform several System 2 tasks simultaneously

As shown in Table 1, our subconscious minds comprise our instincts (avoiding danger), learned responses to stimulus (perceiving hostility in a voice), and automatic tasks learned through repetition or repeated practice (driving a car on an empty road). Functions in our conscious minds require a level of will and intention and come into play when our subconscious programming alone will not do, such as focusing our attention in a crowded room, driving on a rainy day, or paying the bills.

One of the primary functions of our subconscious minds is to make associations between objects and experiences and to provide an instant response, all without involving our conscious attention. This means that every second, our subconscious minds sort through millions of bits of information, categorizing them into relatable chunks that connect to our prior knowledge. Based on that knowledge, our subconscious minds trigger an instantaneous response. When presented with something, our subconscious minds will make a series of associations simultaneously between that thing and other information it holds, centered on three general categories:

1. Cause and effect (virus—cold),
2. Things to their properties (lime—green)
3. Things to the categories to which they belong (pineapple—fruit) (2011, p 52)

Kahneman provides an example of the power of associated responses with the words *banana* and *vomit*. (I know this isn't a pleasant association, but it does make a point!) Without conscious thought, when encountered with that pair of words, we recall memories and experiences associated with each word that produces physiological and mental responses unconsciously— both to the words individually and in relationship to one another. As a result, our neutral or even positive response to bananas becomes influenced by our negative experience of vomit, producing a temporary aversion to bananas—all of which is happening at a speed not registered or controlled by our conscious minds (pg. 50).

Priming is another example of our associative response; when you become predisposed to something without the conscious decision to do so. Kahneman (2011) provides two examples of this phenomenon. First, he gives an example of word association. If we are asked to fill in the missing letter in the word: S O _ P, and if we had just heard the word EAT recently, whether consciously or unconsciously, we would fill in U for SOUP. If we had heard WASH, we would fill in A for SOAP (pgs. 52-53). While we did not consciously register hearing EAT or WASH, our subconscious minds did, and then made the appropriate associations to fill in the missing letter.

In a second example, Kahneman cites a study from New York University. In this study, subjects were asked to form a sentence with the words: Florida, forgetful, bald, gray, and wrinkle. Not only did the subjects automatically associate the words with being old, but the pace of their walking immediately after completing the task was slower than those asked to form a sentence from words not associated with the elderly (2011, pgs. 52-53). Just thinking about the elderly produced an unconscious response in the subject's bodies that caused them to mirror the physical state of being older! We'll come back to priming later in the book as we can intentionally use it to rewire some of that subconscious programming we're walking around with.

> **Big Idea #2:**
>
> Our subconscious minds make associations and decisions based on our prior knowledge, often without our conscious awareness.

While the two minds have different roles, they form a powerful team. Lipton demonstrates this through a simple example:

> "Operating together, the conscious mind can use its resources to focus on some specific point, such as the party you are going to on Friday night. Simultaneously, your subconscious mind can be safely pushing the lawnmower around and successfully not cutting off your foot or running over the cat—even though you are not consciously paying attention to mowing the lawn" (2008, p. 138).

This is multi-tasking at its best! While the conscious mind is considering what outfit you're going to wear to the party, the subconscious mind is monitoring the full scene—taking in sensory information to ensure that you do not run into any obstacles (your foot or the cat) *and also* performing the learned physical tasks involved with mowing the lawn.

The two minds also work together in learning complex behaviors that then become integrated into the subconscious mind, such as driving a car on an empty road. While initially learning to drive required our full attention, through repetition and practice, we eventually become able to perform the basic functions of driving without any conscious thought. Over time, we only need to apply additional focus while driving in more demanding conditions, such as in traffic or on a rainy day.

When our conscious and subconscious minds are not in agreement, however, we can experience both physical and emotional discomfort. This disconnect can occur because of the way that our brains develop. Throughout our childhood and adolescence, our subconscious minds begin storing tons of data to help us assimilate into our community. Through this development, our subconscious minds hardwire "programs" that inform the instantaneous and unconscious responses we have. Our conscious minds, on the other hand, primarily develop during later adolescence, and after many of our learned responses have already become encoded. This means that while it is natural for young adults to consciously choose values and peer groups that are different from their families, all of that original family programming is still there, operating at the subconscious level.

Have you ever caught yourself saying or doing something that one of your parents did, but that you swore you would never do as an adult? Yep, that's your subconscious programming saying hello! I remember the first time that happened to me. I was a young teacher, maybe 24 or so, and I was having my students help clean up the room at the end of the day. The room was a disaster; wads of paper, candy wrappers, and pencil shavings everywhere. I was frustrated that the room was so messy, and I was directing kids here and there, orchestrating the clean-up. Suddenly I looked down, and I saw myself: one hand on my hip, the other pointing out all the places where there was garbage on the floor. Me, bossy as ever, directing everyone where to go and complaining about how I had just cleaned the room in the morning and how could it get dirty so quickly? At that moment, I remember drawing a sharp intake of breath and realizing that I had become my mother! How many times had that same scene played out in my childhood, but with my mom doing the pointing and me running around my bedroom trying to keep pace with her direction? That was a humbling day. The vision of myself as the cool, hip, young teacher was instantly replaced by a dreaded side of my mother!

Here's the good news. While there are traits that we received as children that we want to keep, we are not doomed to repeat those parts that we would prefer to leave behind. Understanding when our subconscious programming and our conscious identities are at odds, and using processes to come back into alignment, is at the core of the self-work that we will be unpacking throughout this book. I've got you!

Make It Yours:

1. Name one or two skills that you had to learn consciously, but have since become a part of your subconscious programming (such as driving a car).
2. What are some of your "mom moments" where you can see yourself repeating patterns, behaviors, or phrases that you learned as a child?

Where the Rubber Meets the Road

Now that we've discussed our subconscious and conscious minds in general, let's take a closer look at one facet of how this programming affects us: implicit bias.

What is Implicit Bias?

The Kirwan Institute for the Study of Race and Ethnicity at The Ohio State University defines **implicit bias** as, "the attitudes or stereotypes that affect our understanding, actions, and decisions in an unconscious manner" (2017, p. 10). Here are some characteristics of implicit biases:

(1) they are unconscious and automatic and activated without a person's control;
(2) they can be positive or negative;
(3) they are pervasive, and everyone has them;
(4) they do not always align with our conscious (chosen) beliefs;
(5) they have real-world consequences in spaces such as education, employment, and criminal justice, and (the great news);
(6) they are malleable, just as they were learned, they can be unlearned (p. 10).

Like other associative responses, implicit bias happens involuntarily, without our conscious awareness. They result from the messages we heard and saw growing up in our families and communities, as well as from the messages we receive from society in general.

Dr. john a. powell is the director of the Haas Institute for a Fair and Inclusive Society. He studies and writes extensively on the impact of implicit bias. In one example, powell draws a connection between the negative connotation of the word "black" in our vernacular and the treatment of African American people in the United States. He says,

> "We looked at 11 million words that most people use over their lifetime, [asking the question, 'How frequently do you use *black* with a negative connotation?']. And it's very high. It's like 40-50 percent of the time. So all the time. That's what you're hearing, that's what you're seeing. It's the air that we breathe. You breathe that until you're an adult, you're going to have those associations. Whites will have them. Blacks will have them. Latinos will have them" (2015).

powell goes on to demonstrate that this same phenomenon can happen with negative associations about women, Muslims, or any other group of people within a society. And importantly, not only do the negative associations affect the viewpoints of people from outside of the target group but also it impacts the self-perception of the people within the group (2015).

Because implicit biases are a part of our subconscious programming, they trigger automatic responses that influence the way that we interpret events, treat groups of people, and see ourselves. They are also a great example of when our conscious beliefs and subconscious programming can conflict. For instance, I consciously believe that men and women are equal. I also have some subconscious beliefs, however, that women are not suitable to hold all the same roles as men, such as leading our military. Why? I've been influenced by the way that the media portrays military leaders, who are almost always male, white, and physically intimidating. When I am presented with the idea of a female military leader, while consciously I am on board, I simultaneously experience a subconscious response telling me women do not belong in that role.

Make It Yours:

Think of one affinity group that you identify with (this could be race, gender, sexual orientation, religion, or any other way you self-identify).

Like my example about women above, what are some ways that this affinity group is portrayed in broader society? Has that portrayal influenced the way you see yourself? Has it affected the way that you treat others in this same group? How?

We come to implicit biases innocently, and they are not necessarily a sign that we are racist or sexist. But it is our responsibility to do something about them. How do we do that? We develop our awareness of when our implicit biases are being triggered, and then we actively make a different choice. The 3 Eyes can help you with this.

Big Idea #3:

Our subconscious minds hold implicit biases that we may not consciously agree with but that nonetheless influence how we view and treat ourselves and others.

Implicit Bias in the Classroom

Our classrooms and schools are microcosms of our larger society. They are the places where biases and stereotypes can get played out and reinforced. They are also the places of most significant potential to address and transform those biases. Ground zero. To take advantage of the potential for profound social change that our schools offer, we need to understand how our cultural backgrounds and implicit biases influence how we teach and interact with our students. We must also become aware of how our students respond to their educational environment based on their cultural norms and beliefs.

Our students of color, our low-income students, our girls, and our students who identify as Lesbian, Gay, Bisexual, Transsexual, and gender non-conforming are particularly vulnerable to the impact of implicit bias. For example, research conducted by the United States Department of Education shows that diversity in schools, including racial diversity among teachers, is beneficial to students, yet our teachers and school leaders remain primarily white (2016). In fact, while the U.S. Department of Education expects that students of color will make up 56 percent of the student population by 2024, the most recent Schools and Staffing Survey (SASS), a nationally representative survey of teachers and principals, shows that 82 percent of public school educators identified as white (2016, pg. 1). The simple fact is that while our student population continues to diversify, our teaching and leadership workforce is not keeping pace, by a long shot.

This is not an attack on white educators, but it does demonstrate the real challenge we have in education. Like all of us, teachers and school leaders harbor subconscious beliefs and programming that reflect their cultural norms. Because the majority of educators have cultural norms that are different from their students, it raises the likelihood that they will unconsciously create educational settings that are not inclusive.

Additionally, all educators, regardless of race or color, are a product of their larger society. As Dr. powell demonstrated in his example above, they hold unconscious beliefs about themselves and their students that reflect the pervasive messages within their society. These biases also play out in the classroom and affect all educators. Dr. Lisa Delpit has been studying and writing about the dynamics of race and culture in the classroom for decades. In her book, *Multiplication is for White People*, Delpit aptly describes America's challenge when she says:

> "The problem is that the cultural framework of our country has, almost since its inception, dictated that 'black' is bad and less than and in all arenas 'white' is good and superior. This perspective is so ingrained and so normalized that we all stumble through our days with eyes closed to avoid seeing it. [As such], we miss the pain in our children's eyes

when they have internalized the societal belief that they are dumb, unmotivated, and disposable" (2012, pp xvii-xviii).

The impact of this cultural framework is undeniable. It can be seen in the discrepancies in wealth, access and power between racial groups, the achievement gap between white and certain Asian subgroups and that of African American and Latino students, and the disproportionate number of African American males in our prison system. Symptoms of our history and ongoing inequities are evident through the social segregation of many of our communities and the prevalence of racial, gendered, and homophobic stereotypes in our media.

Our past has also resulted in the election of our president in 2016 who publicly ridiculed women, the disabled, Mexicans, and Muslims while campaigning. Since taking office, his administration's policies have a pattern of placing power and wealth for the few, over equity and opportunity for all. Political affiliations aside, Donald Trump's election and presidency have coincided with increases in hate crimes in the United States, including in our classrooms and schools. As a white woman who has lived in the progressive bubble of the San Francisco Bay Area most of her life, I have been forced to confront the fact that we have a much farther way to go to live up the ideals that Martin Luther King, Jr. called for in his "I Have a Dream" speech. While I have long understood that inequities exist and have dedicated my career to leveling the playing field, I admit that I did not appreciate the depth of those inequities until now—a sure sign of my privilege and evidence that developing our awareness is a lifelong endeavor.

While our current political and social atmosphere can feel frightening and overwhelming, there is hope. Donald Trump's election and presidency have also coincided with increased political and social activism, and issues of race, gender, sexual orientation, and economic equality have become a part of our national dialogue. From the *Black Lives Matter, Me Too,* and *Times Up* movements, to high school students staging record-breaking nationwide protests to reform our gun laws, we as citizens are stepping forward to change our nation's trajectory. I genuinely believe that this time will represent a turning point in the country towards one that is more inclusive and equitable.

In the midst of our national dialogue, the time has come for discussions about race, culture, and bias to take a more significant place in our classrooms and schools. Eddie Moore et al. note in their anthology, *The Guide for White Women Who Teach Black Boys* (2018), that if we take a systemic approach to addressing racial competence, from teacher training programs to classroom practices, real change is possible. They say, "working together is the only way to create change within a system built on the historical ideology that White is right and Black is wrong. This work is imperative if we are going to change outcomes for Black boys," and by extension, all students impacted by bias (Moore et al., 2018, p. 5). The starting point for this transformation is a sincere to desire to learn, a willingness to understand ourselves and our pasts, and the ability to listen to other's truths.

Glenn Singleton, a leader in addressing systemic educational inequality through what he terms *Courageous Conversations* about race, encourages us to voice our unspoken truths so that we can gain critical racial understandings (Singleton, 2018, xvi). By talking about our experiences with race with people who do not share our backgrounds, we gain new perspectives on one another's viewpoints. Singleton also says that to be able to understand the broader racial narratives within the United States, we must first identify and examine our personal racial narratives (Singleton, 2018, xvii). To know others, we first must know ourselves.

This is where **self-work** and **school-work** meet. Through self-work, we enter into an ongoing process of getting curious about and unpacking the subconscious programming that drives so much of how we show up and treat others. Through **school-work**, we develop the collective capacity necessary to address systemwide change. When considering implicit bias in our schools, this means doing the self-work to understand ourselves, our programming, and our biases so that we can engage with others to address the broader impact of bias within our educational system.

Big Idea #4:

Educators must be supported to understand themselves (their backgrounds, biases, and beliefs), and to enter conversations with their peers about race, culture, and identity.

This is What Self-Love Has to Do with It

The way that we relate to others, and how we respond to the way that others relate to us, run as undercurrents in our lives. They have a profound impact on how we show up, how we perceive our experiences, and how we communicate with others. In educational settings, these aspects also have a significant impact on how our classrooms and schools feel, yet relatively little time and attention are paid to these factors in most of our schools. To create significant and lasting change in our lives and our education system, we need to prioritize our relationships, starting with the one we have with ourselves.

Self-Work and School-Work: The Cycle that Keeps on Giving

We've come to the Theory of Action for the 3 Eyes and the reason why self-work and school-work go hand in hand. Let's start with self-work, which is the process by which we come to know ourselves on a deeper level. It's where we identify and change the harmful narratives that run in the back of our minds and that prevent us from realizing our goals. Self-work also enables us to examine how we show up for our students; both in how we interact with them and in the thoughts and beliefs we have about them. The benefits of engaging in self-work are twofold: the first being personal development and empowerment, and the second the ability to participate in the work to transform our schools. Self-work is the gateway to personal transformation, and the 3 Eyes are the keys.

At the core of self-work is self-care, which means *caring for oneself*. While going to the gym, getting a massage, or sleeping-in are great examples of self-care, without coming to love and accept ourselves, these other elements of self-care will be less effective. This is true because self-care without self-love only addresses the superficial discomforts we feel, but not the root of our suffering. At the root are the negative and disempowering messages we tell ourselves all day, messages that emanate from our subconscious minds.

Another element of self-care is self-compassion. Self-compassion means treating oneself with patience, kindness, and understanding. Dr. Kristin Neff is a self-compassion researcher, author, and professor. She says that self-compassion has three parts: self-kindness, common humanity, and mindfulness (2013). Self-kindness means treating oneself with care and providing comfort to oneself. Common humanity involves seeing our experience as a part of the broader human experience and acknowledging that life is imperfect. Mindfulness means staying in the present moment, including staying with negative and painful emotions. When we practice self-compassion, we use our mistakes as opportunities to soften and be vulnerable. Instead of beating ourselves up, we show ourselves heaps of love. We see our suffering as a part of the collective human experience, and we stay present with our discomfort.

Here's how it works: Imagine that the love of your life has just broken up with you. Instead of spending hours, days or weeks deconstructing the relationship and wondering what you could have done differently to make your beloved stay, you show yourself care. You treat yourself as you would a friend who is going through a break-up. You wrap yourself in a comfortable blanket, and you make yourself your favorite tea, you give yourself a hug. Rather than isolating yourself, you remind yourself that like you, there are thousands of people across the planet who at this very moment are experiencing the same pain. Through this reflection, you realize that you are not alone. Finally, instead of going to a bar for drinks or grabbing a tub of ice cream to numb the pain, you sit with it. You allow the tears to flow and you move through the pain. According to Neff, developing our self-compassion is important because it is linked to reductions in anxiety, depression, stress, over-thinking, perfectionism, shame, and negative body image (Neff, 2013). Not a bad return for being kind to ourselves!

Additionally, research conducted by Juliana Breines and Serena Chen (2012) has shown that having self-compassion increases our motivation to improve ourselves. In their study, they compared the influence of self-compassion to self-esteem in four areas:

- participant beliefs about their ability to change a self-identified area of improvement,
- participant willingness to make amends after making a mistake,
- participant effort to improve their performance on a test they had failed, and
- participant sense of hope to improve their social standing (to be upwardly mobile).

Specifically, Breines and Chen wanted to know how self-compassion, as compared to self-esteem, supported participants to deal with an immediate set back as well as how it changed their behavior moving forward. Imagine that you failed a test a big test. Breines and Chen were looking for the differences in outlook between acknowledging the pain of failing the test without beating one's self up (self-compassion), as compared to listing the many ways that you are a good student despite failing this particular test (self-esteem). They also wanted to know what affect both of those mindsets had on your efforts to improve the score the next time.

Across all areas they studied, Breines and Chen found that having self-compassion had a positive influence on one's sense of possibility to improve and effort to improve. They say, "self-compassion...provides a safe and nonjudgmental context to confront negative aspects of the self and strive to better them. Unlike other approaches to failure that tend to undermine personal growth by encouraging inflated or deflated self-assessments (i.e., self-esteem) ...self-compassion is a more effective method of motivating change" (p. 1140). In short, when we show compassion for ourselves, we are more likely to take action towards changing those parts of ourselves that we wish to change.

Why are self-love and self-compassion essential for educators? Because it is natural for educators to put up their armor; there is not a lot of time or space to attend to personal needs and feelings while teaching a class, running a school, or leading a district. Any teacher knows that even having the chance to go to the bathroom is not a given! Education is a very public profession. It is where you must learn on the job, in front of an often unforgiving audience, be those students, fellow teachers, parents, or supervisors. From the onset of our careers, we are also expected to navigate the balance between being experts and learners. As teachers, we are expected to be able to hold the attention of our students while we are also learning the craft of teaching. As administrators, we are expected to understand the intricacies of leading with little or no prior training beyond what we gained in the classroom. For all, regardless of years of experience, we are expected to continue to hone our skills while on the shifting ground of the wider educational landscape. A landscape where policies and measures of success change regularly, and where funds and training are limited. Added to all of this, we must adapt to meet the needs of our students, who come to us with their own unique strengths and needs; sometimes wildly different ones within the course of the same day.

Given these challenges, it makes sense that many of us close our doors and retreat to private practice (literally and figuratively). It is natural to be wary of opening ourselves to others and their criticisms when the pressures on us are already so high. So, why self-love and self-compassion? Because educators are amazing and deserve to feel that way! This is why self-work is important.

While these are good enough reasons for educators to do the self-work, I'll be honest; I've also got a very big ulterior motive: creating schools where children and adults are welcomed, nurtured, and empowered. What's the connection? By doing self-work, we deepen our self-appreciation and motivation to change. When we feel better about ourselves, we can lower our armor and to open-up to genuinely knowing others. When we understand others better, we can come together as a team to support, challenge, push and hold one another through the process of transforming our schools.

School-work is where we address the issues that are preventing all students from learning at their full potential. School-work comprises addressing the conditions that must be in place to create change, and the change itself. The conditions center on building a culture of trust and accountability amongst staff, students, and community. The change is context-specific and can include things like improving student attendance rates, implementing a new curriculum, or addressing implicit bias.

The 3 Eyes framework supports us through it all. Intellect, Insight, and Intuition provide us with the clarity of sight to identify the areas for change. The self-work and school-work provide the processes for implementing change. Figure 1 shows how self-work and school-work support one another.

Figure 1: The Cycle of Self-Work and School-Work

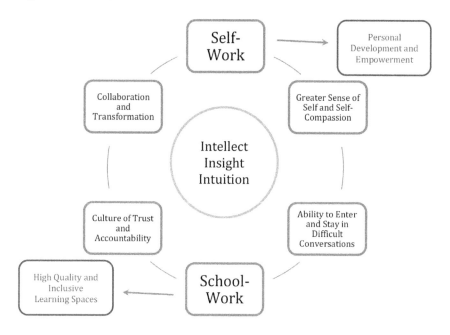

When we engage in self-work, we become more empowered. A byproduct of self-work is a greater sense of self and self-compassion. These attributes enable us to look at ourselves more closely, to receive feedback, and to participate in challenging discussions (about implicit bias and other relevant topics). When we can participate in those conversations, then the groundwork is set to begin the school-work.

Through school-work, we transform our schools into high-quality and inclusive learning spaces for our students. The process of doing the school-work produces more opportunities to deepen our self-work as we learn more about ourselves through the effort of transforming our schools. And on and on it goes.

Throughout, Intellect, Insight, and Intuition give us a means to see ourselves, our educational settings, and our students with more clarity. The self-work and school-work include the processes to implement the changes we seek, and they will be discussed in detail in the final chapter of this book, *Putting it all Together*.

Here then are the theories of action that drive this work:

- **Self-Work:** If we use the 3 Eyes (Intellect, Insight, and Intuition) to see our lives and learned responses with more clarity and embark on a process to lovingly "rewire" the areas that do not align with who we want to be, then we experience greater self-appreciation and motivation to change. When we do that, we can realize our individual goals and engage with others to transform our educational settings.
- **School-Work:** If use the 3 Eyes to identify areas for needed improvement in our schools, and we create communities founded on trust and accountability, then we can use the power of teams to address the areas of needed change. When we do that, we can transform our educational settings into ones that support the adults and students alike to realize their potential.

The cool thing is that by embarking on the self-work, we initiate the school-work. When we create changes within ourselves, it changes the way that we interact with others, automatically adjusting the nature of our educational settings. Like a pebble dropping into a smooth pond, self-work produces a ripple effect. This means that if you are a lone teacher or leader and do not feel like the conditions are in place to do the school-work with a team, the self-work alone will make a difference. Throughout the book, I'll demonstrate how this worked in my own life.

Conversely, if we jump straight to reform side of the school-work without supporting individuals and teams to know themselves and each other on a deeper level, then the conditions will not be in place for systemwide change. Instead, we will continue to produce what we always have, inconsistent and unsustainable school reform. Sure, we'll have bright spots and pockets of real transformation, but they will remain rare examples of what is possible in the midst of a stagnant system that fails more often than it succeeds. I'm focused on succeeding in a big way. The 3 Eyes is the way to get there.

The Warrior's Path

Author, poet, and change leader Margaret Wheatley encourages us to take the Warrior's Path to transform what ails our world. As a part of this path, Wheatley says that we must develop our direct perception and clear seeing. She says,

> "Every one of us constructs a world and then lives inside our personal creation. Without training, we cannot see the richness of information that the world offers us. With practice, we learn to experience moments of direct perception, free of our filters and bias. As we take in more of the world, our habitual filters lose their grip. We see with greater clarity and we also experience the world's innate beauty and luminosity. Our actions become wiser, our compassion deepens, and our commitment strengthens" (2018).

The 3 Eyes framework provides the tools for that training. Through intentional use Intellect, Insight, and Intuition, we learn to see our lives, our habitual responses, and our world with more clarity. Through training in the 3 Eyes (via self-work), we come to see and appreciate ourselves with new depth, which enables us to face the parts of ourselves that we are not proud of or that we are not in conscious alignment with. When our subconscious and conscious minds are more aligned, we can accomplish things not attainable when we are busy waging war within ourselves. This is the opportunity that our self-work provides. This is what self-love has to do with it.

When we train in the 3 Eyes via school-work, we can see one another, our schools, and our structures with more depth and perspective. We also learn to come together as a team, to support one another rather than undermine one another. We become able to look past the superficial fixes to our education system, and instead, collaborate across our schools and communities to address the roots of our educational inequities.

Organizational management experts Peter Senge et al. took on a similar pursuit that is described in the book, *Presence: An Exploration of Profound Change in People, Organizations, and Society* (2004). In this book, the authors explore how deeper levels of learning, other than those that we habitually participate in, can create an awareness of the issues that are a part of the larger whole of whatever challenges we seek to change. They say,

> "All learning is about how we interact in the world and the types of capacities that develop from our interactions. What differs is the depth of the awareness and the consequent source of action. If awareness never reaches beyond superficial events and current circumstances, actions will be reactions. If, on the other hand, we penetrate more deeply to see the larger wholes that generate 'what is' and our own connection to the wholeness, the source and effectiveness of our actions can change dramatically" (2004, pp 11-12).

Our deep awareness is urgently needed to understand how bias and the United States' cultural framework impact our ability to educate our children. Continuing to focus the bulk of our attention on instructional tools like blackboard configurations and content standards, without looking more deeply at the roots of our inequities, will fail to have an enduring impact on outcomes for our youth. We need to get to the heart of our inequities and transform our educational settings from the inside-out.

I'm going to level with you—this is the long game, and this is unquestionably Warrior work. While not a quick fix, if we want to make profound changes in our own lives and in our students' lives, we'll need to be brave and develop our ability see beyond the surface. When we do this, we can access deeper levels of meaning, both about ourselves and the education system. So, let's put on our 3-D glasses and get down to work!

Make it Yours:

1. What do you hope to learn through reading this book?
2. Consider creating your own Theory of Action for applying the 3 Eyes to an area of your life.

A simple frame is: If....then. As a result....

For example: If I approach the content of the book with an open mind, then I will be able to consider ideas that I might otherwise dismiss. As a result, I will be able to stretch my understanding of myself and/or my educational context.

Intellect

"I throw a spear into the darkness. That is intuition. Then I must send an army into the darkness to find the spear. That is intellect." Ingmar Bergman

"We should not pretend to understand the world only by the intellect. The judgment of the intellect is only part of the truth." Carl Jung

Benefits of Using Intellect

Intellect allows us to use the capacity of our brains to make sense of the world, to express our ideas, and to implement the changes we seek. With our intellect, we create amazing things like the Statue of Liberty and the iPhone, as well as to write incredible works of literature and put a man on the moon. Closer to home, our intellect helps us to balance our checkbooks and to move beyond our instinctual responses to make greater meaning of the things we see, feel, and experience. In educational settings, Intellect allows us to do things like create lesson plans, monitor student achievement and teach students how to read. We wouldn't be humans without this lens!

Looking Back

In the previous chapter, we defined Intellect, Insight, and Intuition and learned how together, they allow us to see with more depth, just like when we put on a pair of 3-D glasses. Next, we discussed the interplay between the conscious and subconscious minds and how they shape our reality. In this discussion, we took a closer look at how one element of our subconscious programming, implicit bias, negatively impacts the educational opportunities of many of our students. Finally, we discussed the Theory of Action for the 3 Eyes framework, and how doing self-work alongside school-work is a powerful formula for creating change in individuals and educational settings alike.

Looking Forward

We are now going to discuss education change management; both the processes that support effective change, as well as the conditions that will allow adults to be their most effective at work. We'll start by outlining the basic components that need to be in place when initiating a change in an educational setting. Next, we'll discuss the conditions that must be in place to effectively implement those changes, with a specific focus on creating conditions for individuals to succeed. Much of this content extends beyond the world of education but has common through-lines that I'll apply back to the education context. While some of the concepts we'll discuss may seem out of place with Intellect (we'll get into emotions like love), we are setting a framework for how to create the conditions for change. Intellectually understanding both the technical and interpersonal aspects for creating change are equally important, and we'll cover those in this chapter.

Because the use of the 3 Eyes applies to our personal lives as well as our professional lives, I'll discuss the love-hate relationship I have with my Intellect, and how I finally decided that while we didn't need to start seeing other people, I could no longer commit to Intellect alone. These changes include learning to listen to my heart as well as my head and learning to trust in others.

Glasses frames represent this lens, so let's put on our specs!

You've Gotta Have a Plan, Stan!

Creating change in educational settings is complex, challenging, and completely doable. Successful change initiatives require not only a well-thought-out policy but also a clear implementation plan. Let's define a **policy** as a series of rules and procedures that are focused on a particular goal. Examples of policies in education include the Common Core State Standards, guidelines that govern individual districts, and the way that discipline is carried out at a particular school. We can define a **policymaker** as anyone who creates rules, reforms or long-term plans that affect the core functioning of a system. Any leader who initiates a change can be a policymaker, including state superintendents of public instruction, local superintendents, central office leaders, principals, and teachers. **Implementation** is achieved when the people involved in creating the policy can plan for and execute all of the steps that it will take to get from where they are at present, to where they eventually want to be. **Implementers** are the people who do the work to put the policy in place, and **stakeholders** are anyone affected by the policy, including those who implement it. Linking the stages of implementation together requires three things: forethought, coordination, and a step-by-step action plan.

Forethought: Avoiding the Could-Have's and Should-Have's

Connecting policy and action can be challenging for policymakers because while they may have the overall vision, they do not always have the practical experience or context-specific information to make their ideas come to life. Before initiating a policy, therefore, policymakers should learn all that they can about the current conditions, the people affected by the change, and the potential impact the new policy may have on existing systems and structures.

Diane Ketelle and Pete Mesa are experienced school and district leaders and professors in Educational Leadership. They say that effective policymakers have empathy. They say **empathy** is the ability to assess others' viewpoints accurately, and it is achieved through fact-finding in three specific areas: Time, Context, and Point of View (2006, p. 147). **Time** includes understanding the history of the organization, present readiness to implement a policy, and the future vision of where the organization will be in five years. **Context** includes understanding the norms and values of the organization and the stakeholders. Context also involves gauging the social-emotional climate to assess whether tensions and conflicts (or feelings of community and collaboration) exist that will affect the organization's ability to implement the policy. **Point of view** involves gathering input from diverse stakeholders and reviewing existing research on the potential policy. Sample questions to build our empathy and assess the policy's impact include:

- Are there existing programs or policies that will run in conflict with the new policy? If yes, what parts of the new policy or current policies need to be adapted?
- Do we have staff with the right know-how to put this policy in place? If no, what additional training or support will we need to provide?
- How much will it cost (in terms of time, money, and person-hours) to put this policy in place? Do we have enough people and funding to make it happen and keep it going?
- Do we have sufficient support from our stakeholders for this policy? Who are our champions? Who might we want to engage with further before moving forward?
- Can the current (school or district) climate support a change at this time? Do we need to address an existing tension before taking on the policy change?
- What values are driving this change? Do these values align or conflict with our stakeholders' values?
- What lessons can we apply from past implementation efforts to this new policy?

While putting a new policy in place can have a lot of excitement and urgency behind it, rushing into action without pausing to thoroughly assess the scene can lead to big problems and delays down the line. Questions or needs left unaddressed at the beginning of a change have a way of cropping up eventually, so it is best to bring those out in the open as soon as possible. The adage, "an ounce of prevention is worth a pound of cure," holds true with policy implementation.

Make It Yours:

Pick a change that you would like to see in your context (this could be your classroom, school, department, or district). We're going to analyze it over the next three Make It Yours sections, starting with forethought. I recommend picking something reasonably small so you can get the hang of the steps.

Brainstorm answers to the following questions:

Forethought:

- Time:
  - o What is the history of change in our context?
  - o Has this policy been tried before? Is it new?

- Context:
  - o What are the values that drive your community?
  - o How does this policy align with existing norms and values?
  - o What issue(s) is this policy seeking to address?
  - o Is the timing right for this change?

- Point of View:
  - o Who will be impacted by this change?
  - o What information do you want to gain through talking with stakeholders?
  - o What does the research suggest?

Coordination is for More than Just Dancing

To gather the necessary information and commitment for a change, communication must flow both ways; from policymaker to those impacted by the policy, and back up again (Odden, 1991, Berman & McLaughlin, 1978). Through this reciprocal communication, effective policies are shaped by the vision of policymaker and the practical know-how of implementers. Not only does working with key stakeholders early and often make a policy more likely to succeed, but failing to do so can lead to a lack of buy-in and inconsistent implementation.

Failure to develop a shared vision often occurs because policymakers underestimate the power of individual schools, teachers, and communities to influence a program's success. For example, in schools, principals and teachers have a powerful influence over implementation. They have a margin of discretion that allows them to pick and choose what policies or parts of policies they will put into practice (Lipsky, 1980). This is true because, in many ways, schools and classrooms operate as independent entities. While schools may be a part of a school district and beholden to the district's policies, for example, much of the time it is up to the principal to carry out a district's mandates on their own. The same is true in classrooms. Most the time teachers are alone in their classrooms and can, therefore, stray from their school's norms and routines without much notice. This is not to say to principals and teachers are intentionally subversive, but let's face it, change is hard! When we impose policies without first checking in with those who carry them out, it is difficult to get the necessary buy-in and effort to put the policy into action.

Engagement isn't a one-time event. Gaining buy-in for a policy requires regular communication at every step of the implementation process, especially with those most responsible for putting it in place and those most affected by it. This means that not only should policymakers engage with staff, but also with parents and students. Communication also cannot just be one-sided, where policymakers tell the stakeholders how it's going to be. Instead, there should be a give and take of both information and feedback between policymaker and stakeholders. Policymakers need to be prepared to change their policies based upon the information they receive through the engagement process and as the policy is being rolled out.

This does not need to be a free-for-all, where a policy can change wildly based on the different viewpoints stakeholders bring forward. Policymakers should share the rationale for the policy, what the envisioned change will result from the policy, and what parts of the policy are up for debate and what elements are fixed and are unlikely to change.

As in so many parts of our lives, boundaries are our friends! When policymakers take care at the front end to share the challenges they are seeking to address, and which parts of the policy can change and which cannot, then stakeholders can focus their feedback towards the areas where they have influence. When policymakers gather input on parts of the policy that are unlikely to change or fail to communicate the rationale and expected benefits of the policy, it can erode trust and undermine buy-in. Stakeholders may also experience that their input is not valued or fail to understand why the plan is needed.

> **Big Idea #5:**
>
> Successful change initiatives require ongoing and open communication, collaboration, and flexibility—both on the part of the policymaker and the stakeholders.

Make It Yours:

Please return to your brainstorm for the change you want to implement. Quickly review the work you did on understanding your context through forethought.

As you look at this analysis, consider who should be involved in planning for and implementing the change.

Coordination:

- Key Stakeholders:
  - o Who will be the implementers for this policy?
  - o What is the most effective way to engage with these staff? Students? Families?

- Leading Engagements:
  - o What is the best way to engage stakeholders?
  - o What structures are in place for engaging? What new structures should be established?
  - o How often should you meet?

Put One Foot in Front of the Other

Developing and successfully implementing a policy is an ongoing and dynamic process. I won't kid you; it also takes time. Even if policymakers have done an excellent job engaging on the front end, people need time to adapt to change and to develop a personal interpretation of a policy's significance to their work or lives. Each step of the implementation plan also needs to be carefully thought out and planned so that there is an infrastructure to support the policy's success.

Think of implementing a policy like building a house and the policy is the roof. Without the foundation, support beams, and walls, there would be nothing to put the roof over. The same is true when implementing an educational change. Let's imagine that our *roof* is moving to standards-aligned instruction. Without the foundation and support beams of teacher professional development, curriculum mapping, textbook adoption, and an assessment system, there won't be standards-aligned instruction.

There are experts at each stage of building a house who contribute their knowledge to ensure that the house is stable and strong. The same is true for moving to standards-aligned instruction. People with expertise at each stage of implementation have valuable insights that will lead to successful policy implementation. Content specialists provide input into how and when to teach the standards. The data team helps to create an assessment system to measure student content mastery. Principals support their teachers to teach the content standards in their specific context. Teachers provide input as to what additional information is needed to address their student needs. And so on. Just as a blueprint provides the outline for building a new home, our implementation plan provides the detailed steps for putting the policy in place.

Finally, just as with any construction project, putting a policy in place often takes longer than expected. The more complex the policy and the more people involved with it, the longer it will take to implement (Pressman and Wildavsky, 1979). Educational researchers Paul Berman and Milbrey McLaughlin found in their study of federal education policy implementation that, "any significant innovation or new project in school districts takes about two years to 'get off the ground,' another two years to be fully implemented, and one or two years more to produce a stable effect on student outcomes" (1978, p. 35). In educational settings, expectations that change will occur quickly often leads to criticism of the program or of the teachers and schools attempting to implement it, and this "event mentality" can significantly harm people's motivation and willingness to change (Hall & Hord, 2006, p. 5).

How can we ensure policy implementation is a process rather than an event? We build time into our implementation plan, and we set our expectations accordingly. If a policymaker expects for there to be significant changes in student achievement after the first year of moving towards standards-aligned instruction, for example, they will be disappointed. Instead, if the policymaker were to set concrete goals for student achievement for five years down the line, and then backward-maps what can be accomplished in years one through four, then they have a better chance of achieving their goals. Perhaps in year one, the goal is to develop the curriculum and find textbooks. Year two the goal is to create and beta-test professional development sessions with a subset of teachers and principals. Year three is to refine the content and roll it out to the whole district. Year four is dedicated to further refinement of the material based on student achievement and teacher feedback. If we do these things, then by year five, we have a good sense of whether we have moved to standards-aligned instruction and whether it has benefitted our students.

Make it Yours:

Alright, we're at the last part for developing a plan for policy implementation—goal setting and timelines. While these may seem like obvious and simple steps to take, it is often where policies go astray.

Implementation Plan:

- Timeline:
    o   Five years down the line, what do we hope will be true as a result of this policy?
    o   What can we accomplish in year 1, 2, 3 and 4 that will lead to our goals in year 5?

> - Goal Setting:
>   - o How will we measure our progress on implementing our goals?
>   - o How will we measure progress on student achievement as we build towards our 5-year goal?

Look, I know that time is of the essence, and it is excruciating to slow down when students need better instruction NOW. Nonetheless, decades of research prove that speeding up the process works against our goals. I've worked under numerous superintendents. One of them loved the phrase, "You've got to move slow to move fast." Accordingly, he took the time to build relationships and to think through the steps of policy implementation with a broad group of stakeholders. This leader was masterful at creating excitement and enthusiasm for the changes he wanted to make because he showed that he cared and he appealed to our urgency and passion for making a difference. Through his efforts, those of us that were a part of carrying out the changes became believers, too, and helped to spread the enthusiasm and commitment. As a result, while this superintendent transitioned from leading my district many years ago, many of his programs and policies remain.

I have also worked under a superintendent who loved the phrase, "You've got to move fast to move fast." I know, it seems unlikely that two superintendents would have almost the exact, yet entirely contradictory, catchphrases, but they did! This superintendent led through directives and mandates. He hand-picked a small corps of central office leaders to make most of the decisions. The majority of these leaders also came from outside the district. The superintendent set ambitious goals and established various ways to monitor progress towards those goals. While I believe that his intentions were good and that he wanted to improve outcomes for students, his top-down and accelerated approach undermined his efforts. What he missed in his haste was the context in which he was leading. Without taking the time to get to know the unique history, dynamics, and needs within my district, his policies often drew sharp criticism from our stakeholders and covert resistance from staff. When he left the district, many of his policies were immediately replaced. While we moved fast, we ultimately lost those years and had to start many initiatives over again when the leadership changed.

Bringing us back into the context of the 3 Eyes, Intellect is all over policy implementation! Our intellect allows us to form plans, timelines, and goals. Intellect helps us to map out the steps for implementation and identify the appropriate people to engage with throughout each phase. Intellect helps us to review the research and to select strategies. Intellect supports us to act as an observer and learn from our mistakes. Intellect also helps us to anticipate challenges and adapt accordingly. Intellect helps us to set goals and monitor results. You get the idea. Intellect and policy implementation go together like peanut butter and jelly!

Big Idea #6:

Educational change initiatives take time to be implemented, usually between three to five years. Speeding up the change process often results in resistance and inconsistent implementation.

Let's look at an example. A few years back, I was working with a district to develop their multi-year improvement plan. As a part of that work, I supported the district leaders to look at their data (how their kids were doing in various measures including academic achievement, attendance, and graduation rates), evaluate the effectiveness of their current plan, and identify priorities for the upcoming school year. During this process, I saw that the district planned a significant investment in school counselors. Intrigued, I asked what they hoped to achieve through this investment, and how they were going to measure their results. The leaders said that through investing in more counselors, they expected their annual attendance rate (the percentage of time kids attend school) to improve.

In my mind, I ran through an array of options for how the two connected. Perhaps the counselors would increase the level of safety kids felt, and therefore they came to school more often? Or, the counselors would connect students and families to services both in school and out that would promote improved stability at home, which would, in turn, translate into improved attendance? In actuality, the district leaders envisioned the counselors conducting tardy sweeps. The counselors were also expected to be responsible for more proactive outreach to families about attendance, especially those students who regularly missed school.

This kind of involvement with attendance is not necessarily a traditional role for counselors. I asked if the counselors knew this expectation of them. Not yet. Had they been able to provide input into how it would fit with their other responsibilities? No. Did the district have a plan for training counselors in their new duties and a way to assess their effectiveness at this new task besides end-of-year attendance rates? No.

Before moving forward, the district leaders needed to build their empathy and assess impact. First, they oversimplified the solution to a very real and pressing challenge: student attendance. While counselors could surely play a vital part in improving attendance, usually multiple factors are at play when a child misses school. The district needed more information about the factors that were impacting the attendance rates of students at particular schools and across the district. Once they had gathered more information about their students' needs, the district could determine the best use of their precious resources. It could be that counselors remained the best investment to support students, but it could also mean that there was an alternative intervention that would be more effective.

Next, while the central office leaders had a vision for improving attendance through investment in school counselors, the counselors did not know that they were responsible for improving attendance. Because of this, it was highly unlikely that counselors would focus on attendance in the midst of their myriad of responsibilities. Before proceeding, district staff needed to talk with their existing counselors. How did counselors spend their time now? What priorities drive their work? How do counselors understand their role in improving attendance?

The district also needed additional context about attendance monitoring and improvement efforts at individual schools. For this, the central office leaders needed to talk to some of their principals. What roles currently existed to support attendance? Would the counselor's new role augment current structures or be duplicative? What did principals identify as most important for improving attendance? If they could invest funds in improving attendance, what would they choose?

Finally, the district was in danger of underestimating the time it takes to implement a change. They had set ambitious end-of-year goals for improved attendance after the first year of implementing their new policy. Instead, they needed an implementation plan that also included time to build the new system. Before real changes could be seen in student attendance, the district needed to do a few key things:

- ✓ invest some time in co-creating the role of the school counselor (with school counselors and principals at minimum);
- ✓ hire additional counselors;
- ✓ develop a training for counselors in attendance intervention and provide that training;
- ✓ and develop a means for assessing the impact of their plan at benchmarks along the way.

With forethought, coordination, and detailed planning, the district was able to hone its plan and ensure that all stakeholders (especially the counselors) were on the same page.

Put It Into Action, Jackson

Okay, so what did we learn? Change takes time. It also requires careful, yet adaptive, planning with clear markers for success along the way. Change also requires that folks at every level of the change initiative feel engaged and committed to the change.

So, how do we do that?? Based on my study of experts in change management and on my own experience, putting plans into action requires that we:

1. Value Individuals
2. Build Trust
3. Lean into Love, and
4. Create Spaces for People to Learn, Grow, and Grapple

As you will notice, three of those ingredients are what we might call "soft" skills; to value individuals, to build trust, and to lean into love. They can be felt but not necessarily be seen in any tangible way. The other one is a "hard" skill; create spaces for people to learn, grow, and grapple. This skill requires clear actions and outcomes that can be monitored. While I've broken them apart to explore them in detail, there is more of an ebb and flow to these ingredients as they inform and influence one another. Also, while many of these skills draw upon our emotional intelligence and therefore could easily fit in the chapter on Insight, we're discussing them here because it is helpful to have an intellectual understanding of why they are important. Through understanding them with our Intellect, we can be more intentional about applying them. We're going to start with the soft skills because, in my experience, they are often undervalued by leaders. Make no mistake: they are essential for lasting success.

Value Individuals

A key ingredient for creating change or building a positive work environment is being able to harness the skills and abilities of a wide array of individuals. To do this, we need to be able to build relationships with people from all walks of life and who have viewpoints that may differ from our own. Google has a full people analytics team dedicated to understanding how to hire and support the optimal employee for Google, and there is a lot we can learn from their research. They have found that the most important qualities of Google's top employees included being a good communicator, having empathy towards one's colleagues, and being a good coach (Davidson, 2017). In fact, all of these interpersonal skills were more important than the one that might seem the most obvious for success at Google—expertise in information technology!

Google's people analytics team also studied what makes a good team. After examining the various teams that work at Google (from role-alike to project teams, teams with a lot of diversity to more homogenous), they found that the best teams were ones where team members felt emotional safety. To me, emotional safety is best described by what professor, author and researcher Brene Brown describes as *connection*. According to Brown, connection is the "energy that exists between people when they feel seen, heard, and valued; when they can give and receive without judgment; and when they derive sustenance and strength from the relationship" (2010, p. 19). On the best teams at Google, co-workers built connection by demonstrating emotional intelligence (the ability to recognize one's own emotions and those of others), as well as through generosity, empathy, and curiosity towards their teammates (Davidson, 2017). Why are connection and emotional safety important? When individuals feel seen and valued for being themselves, they feel confident in taking risks, speaking up, and making mistakes (DuHigg, 2016). When they can do that, they can bring their full selves to their teams, and therefore can make a more meaningful contribution.

On the flip side, Google determined that one of the blocks to a more cohesive organizational culture resulted from implicit biases (what they call unconscious bias). Google found that,

> "Unconscious bias can prevent individuals from making the most objective decisions. They can cause people to overlook great ideas, undermine individual potential, and create a less than ideal work experience for their colleagues. By understanding unconscious bias and overcoming it at critical moments, individuals can make better decisions… and build a workforce and workplace that supports and encourages diverse perspectives and contributions" (reWork, 2018a).

Sound familiar? Just as we discussed in the previous chapter, our subconscious minds have a profound impact on how we perceive and respond to others. When we operate with unchecked biases and assumptions, we prevent people from being able to express who they are. They are not safe, and therefore they hold back all that they have to offer.

To develop their employees' understanding of this unconscious programming, Google has developed a voluntary program on implicit bias. It's called "Unconscious Bias @ Work," and it helps employees to understand the concept of unconscious bias and its impact. To date, more than half of the company (30,000 people) has taken this workshop, making it the most popular voluntary program at Google (reWork, 2018b). Google is still in the process of understanding the impact of their Unbiasing program, but they are confident that it will have a profound effect on the company culture as research has proven that being aware of unconscious bias can lead to reversals in biased outcomes (reWork, 2018a).

> **Big Idea #7:**
>
> Individuals need to feel emotionally safe to fully contribute to a relationship, team or larger organizational culture.

There are many implications for Googles' work in the education community. Martin Luther King, Jr. said, "People fail to get along because they fear each other; they fear each other because they don't know each other; they don't know each other because they have not communicated with each other." As Google found out, this failure in communication comes not only from overt messages we confer but also in the ways that we unconsciously evaluate and treat one another. In educational contexts, this means developing our educators' race and cultural competence and understanding of implicit bias. Like Google's Unbiasing program, ensuring that all staff participate in at least annual training on implicit bias is an important start. Supporting teachers and school leaders to extend that training to include culturally responsive teaching practices is another.

This also means that we support adults to build positive connections with one another. I say this with heaps of love, but educators are a judgmental bunch! Perhaps it's because we are trained to evaluate our students' mastery, so we have an eye towards areas of improvement. Perhaps it's because of the urgency we feel to improve outcomes for kids that we put such incredibly high standards on the adults that work with them. Perhaps it's because we are scrutinized so closely by parents, colleagues, and supervisors that we turn that same gaze towards others. Perhaps it is all of these or something else entirely. But man, can educators cut people down and quick!

I know this is true because I have been a source of those judgments towards others, and I have felt the pain when those judgments have been turned towards me. I'll admit to writing off certain colleagues because I didn't think they were cool enough, competent enough, or quick enough to get the job done. I've bypassed my peers and worked around them when I determined that they were not up to the task, whatever that task may be. I've been a part of the cool group whose exclusive membership made others feel like outcasts. I've talked behind peoples' backs and undermined their authority. I'm not proud of it, but there it is.

I've also been on the receiving end—plenty. As a new teacher, I had my ideas and enthusiasm dismissed by senior teachers. I've been told that I'm too emotional and therefore not up to specific roles. I've been cast out of in-groups for reasons I still do not know. I've been shunned for being too opinionated and for setting boundaries with the wrong people. I've gone from being a key decisionmaker with 100's of emails in my inbox (a sure sign of my worth as an employee!) to having next-to-nothing to do overnight. I know first-hand that both sides of the judgment coin feel awful. They also absolutely, 100%, no question, get in our way of making schools the nurturing and empowering places they need to be for our students.

Why? We started this section by describing the qualities of Google's ideal employees and best teams. Those qualities included having empathy, emotional intelligence, and good communication skills. The best teams were ones where staff felt emotional safety. So here's the problem with the judging that we do in education. First, if we are directing those judgments towards others, it also means that we are judging ourselves. Second, both forms of judgment (of self and other) produce feelings of shame and unworthiness. When we feel these things, then we get busy armoring ourselves. We withdraw and close our classroom doors, we attack others, or do any other kind of behavior that helps us to feel safe and in control.

Brene Brown defines shame as, "the intensely painful feeling or experience of believing that we are flawed and therefore unworthy of love and belonging – something we've experienced, done, or failed to do makes us unworthy of connection" (Brown, 2013). If we are feeling unworthy of love and belonging, we shut down. When we shut down, we are not able to engage in the schoolwork, to do the things we need to do to make schools empowering places for kids. Brown also says that shame cannot survive when it is spoken (you tell someone you trust how you are feeling) or when it is addressed with empathy.

Our ability to show empathy and hold the space for other's shame begins with our ability to love ourselves. Brown says, "true belonging only happens when we present our authentic, imperfect selves to the world, [and therefore] our sense of belonging can never be greater than our level of self-acceptance" (2010, p. 26). All roads lead back to self-work! As we begin to love and accept ourselves more, we are better able to extend that same care towards others. In educational settings, this means that we learn to value ourselves so that we can see the value and unique gifts of others. When we can do that, we set the foundation for individuals to feel safe enough to show up and do the vital work of transforming our education system into one that helps our students to love and value themselves.

Make It Yours:

Think of a team you have been on where you felt emotional safety and one where you did not.

- How did your feelings of safety in each situation affect the way you expressed yourself?
- Your willingness to take risks?
- Your level of effort?
- How did it impact your sense of value to the team?

Build Trust

When we create spaces where people feel seen and valued, we also create the appropriate conditions to build trust. Leadership expert and author Stephen M.R. Covey has done extensive research on the role that trust plays in our personal and professional relationships, and he says that being able to establish, grow, and restore trust is the key leadership competency of the new global economy. According to Covey:

> "Trust is one of the most powerful forms of motivation and inspiration. People want to be trusted. They respond to trust. They thrive on trust. Whatever our situation, we need to get good at establishing, extending, and restoring

trust—not as a manipulative technique, but as the most effective way of relating to and working with others, and the most effective way of getting results" (2006, p 29).

Why is this so? Trust builds confidence, while the opposite, distrust, breeds suspicion. Without trust, we do not feel safe. As discussed above, if we do not feel safe, we do not bring our full selves to our work or relationships.

Our need for trust is rooted in our subconscious programming. Professor of psychology David DeSteno studies the role of trust in relationships. He says that trust is so important because needing to trust others means that we are vulnerable and that the ability for us to obtain what we need or desire is not entirely within our personal control (2014). When there is a lack of trust, we feel vulnerable and unsafe. Our brains experience this as a threat and send us into fight or flight mode—we shut down, cannot perform at our best, and respond with either aggression or retreat.

In educational settings, trust is vital between coworkers, between staff and families, and between staff and students. Coworkers must rely on one another to do their part to keep the system working and students learning. Parents entrust their children to a school's care in the belief that their children will receive the best possible education. Students place their futures in educators' hands and rely on them in order to be prepared for college, career and beyond. Trust is important!

Trust is a result of two things: character and competence. *Character* includes one's integrity and motivations. *Competence* comprises one's skills, abilities, and achievements (Covey, 2006, p. 30). While character is an enduring quality (it is with us in all situations), competence is situational. Both are crucial because while the character side can build positive feelings, when we are seeking help or guidance (in other words, when we are vulnerable), we want to work with people who also have the proven results and skills to back up all that integrity (Covey, 2006). DeSteno (2014) asserts, "good intentions, without the ability to bring them to fruition, don't count for much in the end" (p. 30). DeSteno goes further and cites research that shows that our minds rapidly capture signals of a person's social standing (i.e., status) and expertise (ability to do the job at hand) within milliseconds (2014, p 31). This split-second assessment affects the level of trust we ultimately give to others. There goes the subconscious mind again!

Building trust in our schools and districts requires that we are open, honest, and accessible. Imagine that I am a principal of a low-performing school and I have some ideas for how to improve student achievement. To gain buy-in for those changes, I need to be honest with my community about the challenges that exist in the school and why I think my solutions will help. I need to tell my teachers that the way we have been educating our kids is not having the desired results. I need to tell parents that we have not adequately prepared their children for the next grade. I need my full community to see the challenges so that we can work together toward a solution. Let me tell you, this can be painful and difficult, but it is essential.

Not only is it important for me to be open and honest, but I also need to communicate in a way that ensures I am understood. Covey encourages us to stick to the facts and take responsibility for our part in any areas we want to change. Attempting to downplay, sugar coat, or deflect blame for my school's failings would only succeed in diminishing trust between myself and my community (Covey, 2006). Instead, I need to create transparency by telling the truth in a way that is open, authentic and can be verified (p. 157). I also need to share this information in a way that is accessible and appropriate to my audience. While with my teachers, I may use pedagogical terms and other insider language, when I am addressing parents, I need to remove the edu-speak and explain terms that may not be familiar to a layperson.

Finally, being transparent requires that I regularly communicate about the outcomes my school is achieving (or not), as we attempt to solve the problem. My community needs to know when and how to get in contact with me. They need a clear calendar of school transformation events with dates several weeks in advance so they can arrange to be there. They need to know how we are progressing towards our goals and whether we are achieving the results we expected that we would. They need the implementation plan to be in place, so they know what to expect and when.

Character and competence are also crucial for our interpersonal relationships. As we've discussed, to trust others, we need to feel emotional safety. We need to know that we are seen and supported for who we are and that we will not be cast out of our tribe if we show our flaws. This kind of trust is built over time and through our actions. Brene Brown (2012) uses a great analogy of a marble jar to demonstrate how to build trust. In one of her daughter's classes, her teacher used a marble jar as a class incentive—if the collective group followed the classroom's norms, the teacher added marbles to their jar. If the class broke the classroom rules (such as misbehaving with a substitute), then marbles were taken away. Once the marbles reached the top of the jar, they got a party. Brown used this analogy to help her daughter evaluate which of her friends were worthy of her trust and vulnerability—what they called her marble jar friends. Brown's daughter's marble jar friends were those who demonstrated in a lot of little ways that they cared for her (such as knowing her grandparents' names, when her brother was sick, or what her afterschool schedule was like) (2012).

Building trust in our personal and professional relationships works the same way. Rather than jumping in with our full vulnerability and sharing the significant parts of ourselves with our friends and co-workers (starting them with the entire jar of marbles), we build trust over time. Marble by marble, we build relationships and assess whether or not folks have earned the right to our stories, and whether or not we can be emotionally safe with them. We earn others' marbles when we demonstrate our trustworthiness. This is achieved by how well we show empathy and compassion towards our friends and colleagues. By how well we suspend our judgments and seek understanding instead. By how well we take care to know each other's stories, the big things and the more mundane. How many kids does my colleague have? What are their names? How does my co-worker like her coffee?

Perhaps by now, you knew I was going to say this, but part of the trustworthiness we need to build is with ourselves. Iyanla Vanzant is a spiritual teacher and life coach. According to Vanzant, we must learn to trust ourselves and our judgments before we can extend that trust to others. She says that self-trust is the "unwavering, unquestionable inward conviction about your value, worth, and ability to be, to create, and to enjoy all that you desire in the process of living and learning more about yourself" (2015, p. 11). The 3 Eyes help us to see ourselves and our lives with more clarity. Self-work provides the process to build our self-love and our ability to trust ourselves.

Big Idea #8:

Trust is a necessary component to all relationships, both personal and professional. We build trust through our character and our competence.

Make It Yours:

What are some of the ways that others demonstrate their trustworthiness to you (your marble jar moments)? What actions can cause you to remove marbles (trust)?

What are some ways you have come to trust yourself? What are some examples of how you break trust with yourself?

Lean into Love

Building the trust and emotional safety described above has implications in various parts of successful education transformation. Emotional safety enables people to let down their guards and bring their full selves to their work. Trust is important for marshaling the collective will to implement a policy, especially when the going gets tough. When I say *Lean into Love*, then, the encouragement is to create those spaces where staff feel seen, valued, and safe. Spaces where people take the risk to make mistakes, speak their minds, and be vulnerable.

The opposite are workplace cultures where people openly express harsh criticism toward one another or talk behind each other's backs. They are places where implicit biases run unchecked. These kinds of cultures create a toxic atmosphere that undermines reform efforts before they ever get off the ground.

When we *lean into love*, we create spaces where individual and group accomplishments are celebrated, where there is space for open and spirited dialogue and where people know more about each other than their job title. The love I am speaking about has its roots in compassion. **Compassion** can be defined as suffering with or relating to the pain of, others. Buddhist nun and author Pema Chodron says in her book *The Places That Scare You* that, "compassion is not a relationship between the healer and the wounded. It's a relationship between equals. Only when we know our own darkness well can we be present with the darkness of others. Compassion becomes real when we recognize our shared humanity" (2001, p. 50). The love we need to cultivate, then, begins with our willingness to know and love ourselves. That's the self-work, my friends. By engaging in self-work and developing a deeper level of love and compassion for ourselves, we can connect more deeply with others. We recognize our shared humanity and approach each other with more compassion and care. Imagine what we could accomplish if we approached one another with this kind of love?

In educational settings, we foster love by addressing the general culture of the organization as well as by attending to individual needs. The self-work and school-work cycle! Michael Fullan is an educator and researcher in education reform. He cites examples from business and educational fields to reinforce the notion that while having an organizational moral purpose is essential (for educators, this means ensuring that students are successful), the needs and fulfillment of employees are equally important (2008). Fullan says the key to loving our employees is enabling them to, "learn continuously and to find meaning in their work and in relationship to coworkers and to the company as a whole." (2008, pg. 12). This means, for example, that a teacher's personal goals and development are nurtured *simultaneous*ly to that of their students. This is not the norm in most school districts where the focus on students causes the adults that support them to feel undervalued. Fullan cites evidence from his own school district where they adopted a policy that invested in teachers' development alongside that of their students. Within just a few years of adopting this policy, not only did student reading scores steadily improve, but teacher attrition rates (the number of teachers leaving the profession) also decreased (Fullan, 2008, 35).

My own experiences reinforce what Fullan found in his school district. In many settings that I have been in, there has been a pervasive judgment and frustration that our schools and districts focus too much on *adult problems* (such as pay, working conditions, and sense of belonging), rather than on our kids. I'll admit that I have been guilty of this kind of judgment myself. Let's be clear; children must be the focus of the outcomes we hope to achieve. At the same time, however, I have come to realize that if the adults do not feel safe, seen, and supported, then they will not be able to focus on the needs of their students.

There is an analogy about airplane oxygen masks that aptly demonstrates Fullan's point. At the start of every airplane ride, passengers are instructed that in case of emergency, parents are to put the oxygen masks on themselves before putting them on their children. Parents are told to do this because if they sacrifice their need for oxygen as they attempt to help their child, they may become incapacitated even before they can finish helping their child, and both parent and child become endangered. If we take Fullan's advice to heart, and I do, this means that we support our staff, teachers, and principals to put the oxygen masks on themselves through professional development, coaching, and meaningful engagement before (or at least simultaneously) to asking them to attend to their students. We support our educators to do self-work so that they are poised to engage in the school-work. Getting into a push and pull between adult and student needs, therefore, only succeeds in undermining our ultimate goals for students.

Big Idea #9:

Love your employees through recognition, encouragement, and providing opportunities for personal and professional growth.

If I haven't convinced you that a positive work environment is crucial to effective change management, there is a growing body of scientific research to back me up! Barbara Frederickson is a positive psychologist who studies the impact that positive emotions (such as gratitude, love, and joy) have on our health and well-being. Through her research, she has been able to prove that when we feel good, we can integrate new information faster, think in more dynamic ways, and identify solutions to challenges we may not otherwise have considered (2003). Frederickson's research has found that "even though positive emotions and the broadened mindsets they create are themselves short-lived, they can have deep and enduring effects. By momentarily broadening attention and thinking, positive emotions can lead to discovery of novel ideas, actions, and social bonds," which would otherwise have gone unnoticed (Frederickson, 2003, p. 333). In other words, happy staff are far more creative, collaborative, and open to new ideas. When it comes to making the lives of our students better, intentionally creating positive work environments for our staff translates into a clear win-win scenario for our kids.

Learn, Grow, and Grapple

When we assume that we've done an excellent job of establishing trust and have helped our employees to feel valued and encouraged to grow, then it's time to create some structures to put all those good vibes to use. If you recall, successful policy implementation is both top-down and ground-up. On the ground-up side, Fullan (2008) has found that the use of positive peer groups has far more influence on a policy's success than whether employees fear (or love) the person leading the charge (the top-down side). Said another way, the extent to which people in like-roles feel bonded to and pushed by each other is more important than their relationship to their supervisors. Accordingly, Fullan says that the job of leaders is to provide clear direction while focusing implementation through peer groups.

A well-established way to foster those bonds is through Professional Learning Communities (PLCs). PLCs are peer groups that share best practices and strategies to address a common problem. Use of teacher-based PLCs has been a widespread and research-supported practice in schools for some time, and one that has had proven success in creating the positive peer pressure that Fullan espouses. Educational researcher Mike Schmoker agrees, and notes that, "when teachers engage regularly in authentic 'joint work' focused on explicit, common learning goals, their collaboration pays off richly in the form of higher quality solutions to instructional problems, increased teacher confidence and...remarkable gains in [student] achievement" (Schmoker, 2005a, p. xiii). Many minds are greater than one!

To leverage the power of the PLC, both Fullan (2008) and Schmoker (2005b) encourage the use of learning cycles. In these cycles, PLCs review data and identify a problem they want to solve. They then create a plan to address the issue, implement it, and evaluate the results. This process is called a Cycle of Inquiry (COI), and when these cycles start going, teachers have the opportunity to learn alongside their kids. Through PLC-led cycles of inquiry, teachers strengthen their instruction and become better teachers overall. And, in our cash-strapped educational settings, the awesome news is that "the use of PLCs is the best, least expensive, most professionally rewarding way to improve school" (Schmoker, 2005b, p. 137). We'll talk about the use of these learning cycles in the final chapter of this book and provide examples for how to establish COIs for both professional and personal purposes.

Big Idea #10:

Collaborating with one's peers through PLCs is an effective and professionally rewarding way to create changes that will benefit students.

While PLCs are an excellent way to improve teaching practices, they are not only for teachers. Fullan (2005) says that because the power of PLCs is to engage in disciplined inquiry and continuous improvement, people in every level of the education system would benefit from peer-based learning. Fullan's "tri-level solution" envisions PLCs at the school, district, and state policy levels that intentionally harness the power of group learning to engage in continuous improvement dedicated to student achievement (2005).

Widespread use of PLCs is taking hold. In my district, we have provided our principals with groups of peers to meet and learn with, and we are trying to operationalize a more formal PLC structure centered on COIs. Central leaders also meet regularly, and we are starting to do at least mid-year reflections and changes to our practices similar to a COI. On the state level in California, our new way of funding schools and districts almost requires an annual cycle of inquiry. There have been discussions (although no formalized structures yet) of creating learning communities of district superintendents akin to PLCs across the state. And finally, philanthropy is also getting in on the game. The Bill and Melinda Gates Foundation (one of the biggest philanthropic funders in education) has identified the use of learning networks as one of its core strategies for 2018 and beyond (2017). PLCs do not need to be face-to-face either. With the increased use of online learning platforms, there is real potential for PLCs to be at a global level. I have participated in online learning groups for topics outside of education, and I can attest first-hand that real transformation is possible through remote group learning.

A Tale of Two Teams

PLCs aren't just for the educators in our system. Group learning is a powerful modality to enhance anyone's reflection and growth, whatever the context. Since we're talking about education here, however, below is an example of another powerful way to use PLCs at schools that do not involve teachers.

About ten years ago, I had the opportunity to be an assistant principal at a school designated for transformation. I joined the school in January of the year in which the transformation work had begun. My primary job was to be the administrator at the school site while the principal and the other assistant principal attended professional development on the transformation process off-site. My first solo day in charge was on my fourth day at the school. I was terrified! With only three other days on campus under my belt, I barely knew my way around the campus, let alone the staff, students or procedures of the school.

Nonetheless, there I was, going it on my own. I had the principal's cell phone number programmed into my phone in case of emergencies. Wouldn't you know that other key staff were also away that day? This included the math coach who had been the administrator in change before I got there. And, to add insult to injury, it was a rainy day!

Anyone who has worked at a school knows that rainy days are incredibly taxing on the adults and invigorating for kids. This is a bad combination. Many of a school's normal routines must be changed on rainy days, including recess and lunch times and teacher breaks. Having only been at the school for three days, I knew none of the actual procedures, let alone the special ones for rainy days. Even more importantly, I hadn't had the opportunity to build relationships with any of the staff yet, and they were still sussing me out.

So it's raining, and it's lunchtime. Our school had a tiny cafeteria that was soon to be remodeled, so we had a rotating cafeteria schedule which got classes of kids in and out in three shifts of 20 minutes each. On sunny days, kids would move through the cafeteria to eat and then went outside for recess. No one had to tell me that when it's raining, there is no outside recess. With the first group of kids already in the cafeteria, I had some quick figuring to do, so I started asking around about what procedures were in place. From the cafeteria staff, I learned that during rainy days, kids were taken to the auditorium instead of outside. I learned from the custodian how to get to the auditorium through a hallway that I hadn't yet explored. It allowed us to get kids to the auditorium without going outside. I asked the School Security Officer (SSO) what the kids did in the auditorium. She said that they usually watched a video, but she didn't know where the equipment was. She also indicated that her back was hurting her and she couldn't walk the kids back and forth to the auditorium. Oh boy. I had to get the kids to form lines and walk from the cafeteria to the auditorium, but I had no staff support to get them there and no idea what to do with them once in the auditorium.

I decided not to worry about the auditorium issue yet. I needed to get the first group of kids out of the cafeteria as the second group was already on its way. Looking around for help, my eyes landed on a third-grade girl who I had instantly bonded with on my first day. Trudy was small, fierce, and not afraid to speak her mind. I deputized Trudy as my number two and asked her to walk the lines of kids to the auditorium where the SSO would receive them. Off Trudy went, getting tables of kids to line up. Yes, I had put my trust in this tiny (and I mean small!) eight-year-old girl to transport line after line of kids to the auditorium safely. While it sounds crazy, that was probably the best decision I made that day! Trudy was on fire! All the kids arrived at the auditorium safely, and no one gave her a hard time.

I took the last group over, and when I walked into the auditorium, it was absolute chaos. I don't know what I expected of a group of elementary school kids on a rainy day in a confined space, but I wasn't prepared for what I found. Kids were running everywhere, and there stood the SSO, leaning against the auditorium stage with a wry smile on her face. I did my best to restore order, but the kids were like popcorn kernels; popping up off the floor here and there around the room. Once I got one part of the room settled down, another would start popping. While I have a good, strong teaching voice, most of the students couldn't hear me above the din. Even the ones that could didn't know me, so it was hard to convince them to sit still. It was getting dangerous!

Soon, the custodian came to join the SSO, and the two of them stood there watching me. In desperation, I finally decided it was safer for the kids to go outside, so I released them out into the rain. Just as I let the kids out, the cavalry came! The math coach had returned and quickly gathered the kids back into the auditorium. She was able to restore order in about five minutes flat. I was humbled. Not the illustrious start I had envisioned for myself. Since the kids were safe and relatively dry, no real harm was done. The principal had a good laugh when she heard how my day went and immediately trained me on the procedures.

Flash forward to a year later, and things could not have been more different. As you might imagine, I reflected a lot on that failure. I knew that I needed to get in good with the support staff and quick! To that end, while the principal and other leadership team members focused on creating teacher PLCs, I created a support staff PLC consisting of the administrative assistant, lead custodian, SSO, and yard staff. Together we met on a regular basis to discuss how the school was going, to solve problems, and to collectively address the challenges each encountered in their roles. We did everything from implementing our new yard policies to fire drills to addressing student behavior issues. We also learned about each other's lives. I found out that the SSO was raising her grandsons and that the yard monitor was worried about her son's ability to make friends. The administrative assistant and I shared about our desire to have children and bonded over past relationship troubles. In other words, we put a lot of marbles in each other's jars.

While initially, I saw value in building bonds with the support staff for sheer survival, I came to appreciate the vital role they played in the success of our school. The support staff PLC proved to be so impactful that we formalized its structure and integrated the team's expertise more and more into the major decisions we were making for the school's transformation.

Case in point: the cafeteria. As I mentioned, the cafeteria was due for an upgrade, which meant that we needed to repurpose the auditorium as the cafeteria for about six months. The district's Facilities department had devised a plan for doing this, and one day they came to our school to go over plans with the principal, the other assistant principal, and me. As we walked around the auditorium, the custodian came in and observed our conversation. I don't recall why we didn't include her in the walkthrough, but it was an oversight.

The custodian waited for the district team to leave, and then took the principal and me back to the auditorium. She walked through the plans with us again, pointing out a few key trouble spots, and suggested alternatives. Her ideas helped us to make more efficient use of the auditorium and to avoid some pitfalls that the facilities team had not anticipated.

What a difference a year had made! While initially, staff felt alienated and leery of me and the rest of the new leadership team, we had managed to develop a level of trust and collegiality where they now felt empowered and engaged. They felt a sense of ownership over the school and its success and knew that their perspective was valuable.

Implications

There is a great deal of research on what makes creating change in educational settings effective. There is likewise a mountain of research on other topics in Education, including how to teach specific subjects, what content students should learn, how to plan successful lessons, and on and on. We are not bereft of the knowledge we need to teach our kids or change our systems. While there are certainly bright spots where real change and equitable outcomes for kids are happening, we continue to have a profound achievement gap between student subgroups. The fact is that creating educational settings that are empowering for all of our kids requires more than the faithful implementation of research-based strategies. We need to understand our students' needs, and the challenges we face in our current education system, through all 3 Eyes. Additionally, we must develop our capacity to work with one another while we also address those areas of needed change.

Use of our Intellect has a vital part to play in this transformation. As discussed in this chapter, Intellect provides us with the know-how to evaluate our settings and identify areas of needed improvement. Intellect also supports us to develop and roll-out multi-year implementation plans with aligned goals. By using our Intellect, we can understand how elements like bias, emotional safety, and interpersonal skills impact an individual's ability to engage in change. Intellect also helps us identify the conditions that need to be in place as we embark on transforming our educational settings. Below are some specific implications for both the self-work and the school-work as they relate to Intellect.

Self-Work:

Whether policymaker or stakeholder, creating effective change requires that we come into a deeper and more loving relationship with ourselves. As we begin to love and trust ourselves more, we can extend the same to others, creating the conditions for our colleagues to feel safe, seen, and supported. This is the fertile ground for true transformation and innovation.

As will be discussed further in the book, our Intellect also provides us with the ability to step out of our thoughts and reactions and act as an observer. We can then use our conscious attention to redirect our energy towards acquiring the experiences and goals that we want.

School-Work:

When staff experience emotional safety and collegiality, they can bring their full selves to their work. This safety and collegiality will lead to new levels of collaboration and innovation amongst teams. To create those safe spaces, we must train employees about the elements of effective teams and how to form them. We also need to train all employees to detect subconscious programming and how it affects their outlook, particularly implicit biases.

When initiating a policy change, from the onset, policymakers must include the voices of those impacted by the proposed changes. When this is done, through mutual-adaptation and shared problem-solving, policymakers and stakeholders can work together to implement the policy. This kind of policy implementation takes time, coordination, and thoughtful communication.

Intellect: Friend and Foe

I should start by saying that for most of my life, I have been firmly in the Intellect camp. I am naturally a systems-thinker, and I gain a great deal of comfort and satisfaction from mapping out complicated processes in a logical, linear fashion. I lean on my intellectual skills every day. My systematic and process-oriented thinking is probably evident as you read this book. If you were to look into my head, you'd see color-coded and annotated files with typed tabs. Very neat and orderly.

Given my heavy reliance on my Intellect, I get a huge kick out the fact that I've decided to turn in my Spock ears for the groovy glasses I talk about in this book. In fact, I was so firmly entrenched in my habitual patterns and way of moving through the world that it took not one, but three, significant bumps in my professional career to wake me up. Oy.

As we've discussed so far, our subconscious minds develop in response to our upbringing and early life experiences. They run without our conscious awareness. Part of the subconscious programming I unwittingly developed as a child included beliefs that being vulnerable and relying on others was a no-no.

From a very young age, I learned to be self-sufficient (I potty trained myself as a toddler), and I developed the habit of isolating myself in my mind, sorting things out on my own. These habits formed in response to dynamics in my family and to growing up in Berkeley in the '70's. The flip side of being encouraged to have an independent mind meant having to do a lot of things independently, including taking care of myself and solving my own problems. For me, being able to manage that level of self-sufficiency meant that there was no room for weakness, which I correlated with being vulnerable. For example, one of my strongest childhood memories is from when I was eight years old, and I talked myself out of crying during the final scenes of E.T. I can still place myself in the theater, sitting next to my dad, repeating over and over in my mind, "This is not real. E.T. does not exist in real life." While tears were liberally flowing down my dad's cheeks, the idea of being "caught" crying like that felt like the height of humiliation. There wasn't room for crying or mushiness. My job was to be tough.

I'm not complaining or trying to sound like a martyr. My self-sufficiency and logical mind have served me well, but they've also made me isolated and lonely. Probably most significant for our discussion here is that I had an inherent fear that everything would fall apart unless I stayed constantly vigilant. Whenever I encountered a problem or challenge, my Intellect was there, helping me to think a way through it. I'd jump right in my head and try to visualize the worst-case scenario of whatever was troubling me, and then figure out how I would survive it in painstaking detail. When I wasn't playing that terrible game, I'd run through full arguments with people in my head. Sometimes, I'd talk myself into resolutions to conflicts I was having with others, all without even letting the other person know that I was upset! While I did this to establish some sense of safety and control, all it did was push me into a reactive and highly anxious state of mind.

By age 40, these habits had succeeded in driving a wedge between myself and many of the people I cared about the most. While I was vaguely aware this was happening, I wasn't motivated to do anything about it until a series of setbacks at work. Before my "professional bumps," my workplace goals and relationships meant more to me than my personal ones (except for my son). All of that changed when a crisis in my professional life led to a personal breakthrough.

Going Three for Three

I was laid off for the first time in 2013. And then again in 2014. And again in 2015. In 2013, California was nearing the end of a multi-year economic recession where funding for public education had been steadily cut, forcing school districts across the state to tighten their belts by eliminating staffing and programs. This was true for my district as well, so my job loss was not unusual for the time. Many of my colleagues were also let go as my school district made some difficult decisions about what programs to prioritize and which staff had the skills they needed to do the work ahead. I was laid off after having done some pretty important work for my district, and I had thought that all of my hard work would have earned me a spot on the "keepers" side of the equation. When the layoff came, therefore, I was utterly blindsided and aggrieved.

To make sense of this personal tragedy, I jumped into my head and used my Intellect to sort things out. As such, the final few months between receiving the layoff notice and completing my last day on the job were an emotional roller coaster. Depending on the thought or line of reasoning dominating the day, I either felt angry and victimized or wholly responsible and at fault. I figured that if I could pinpoint where I went wrong, I could avoid it happening again. Rather than attending to my feelings of loss and showing myself some compassion, I spent those final months going over various meetings and interactions I had had with other staff in my district. What could I have said differently? Who had I wronged? Why was my name on the list but not others? As a result, I ended my time in my district with a cocktail of emotions—anger, self-righteousness, self-loathing, fear, sadness, and humiliation. Mind you, I wasn't attending to those feelings; I was suppressing and avoiding them, making me feel numb and bone tired. A great way to start a new job, right?!

Nonetheless, that's precisely what I did. Twice more. The details of jobs two and three mirror much of what was true in job number one. In each, I put my full effort into my work, produced strong results, and then lost my jobs as my organizations' priorities changed. Also in each, I assumed full responsibility for the circumstances that led to my job losses, completely ignoring the broader contexts that included changes in leadership and continued financial constraints. With each job loss, my shame, humiliation, and self-doubt mounted.

Just as my third job was winding down, the school district that had laid me off two years previously recruited me to come back. So, I packed up my boxes (again) and rode my emotional roller coaster back to my school district. While I was grateful to return to the colleagues and friends I had known for up to twenty years, my self-confidence was at an all-time low. I was stuck in my head, trying my best to make sense of all that had happened to me. The stress that my over-thinking was causing me was evident in the dark circles under my eyes and with the tightness in my chest—tightness so powerful that it sometimes became difficult to breathe.

My husband at the time, Richard, knew my pattern well. He saw my pain and the toll that the self-abuse was taking on me. Richard was incredibly patient and kind, and over the previous three years had practically begged me to see that these transitions were not all about me. There were circumstances and other people that contributed to each of the layoffs. Somehow, after that third transition, Richard helped me to see my pattern: overreliance on my Intellect, extreme self-criticism and efforts to control my circumstances through pure will. For the first time, I was able to step outside of myself to see my destructive cycle as an observer. What I saw made me incredibly sad.

With this new and very fragile perspective, I felt lost and groundless. It was the final straw in the growing mistrust I had of my mind. While I could finally see just how profoundly my mind was playing tricks on me, I also didn't know any other way to be. Who was I without my logic? If these circumstances weren't all about me, what did that mean about the control I exerted on my life? If I couldn't use my mind to steer me in the right direction, what else did I have? With such deeply entrenched habits, how could I possibly change them?

What I desperately wanted at that moment was to talk to my dad. While I generally did not ask for help or show vulnerability, he was someone in whom I could confide my deepest fears and worries. He was my rock, the person who always made me feel better and who assured me that things were going to work out. He was able to see through my tough façade to the little girl who was afraid to cry during E.T. He could jar me out of my head and bring me back into my feelings with a joke or by showing his own vulnerability. The only trouble was, my father had passed away ten years before.

There I was, finally ready to make changes, but the person I knew could help me to do it was no longer there. I didn't know what to do, so I just sent out a silent wish to speak to my dad and told him I missed him. Then, I got back to work.

Insight

"Somehow our society has formed a one-sided view of the human personality, and for some reason, everyone understood giftedness and talent only as it applied to the intellect. But it is possible not only to be talented in one's thoughts but also to be talented in one's feelings as well." Lev Vygotsky

"If you want to awaken all of humanity, then awaken all of yourself. If you want to eliminate suffering in the world, then eliminate all that is dark and negative in yourself. For truly, the greatest gift you have to offer humanity, is your own transformation." Lao Tzu

Benefits of Using Insight

We can define **insight** as having a deep understanding of a person or thing. Insight's superpower is that it prepares us to be our best, most aligned and empowered self in the present moment by giving us perspective on how we experience our reality. Insight helps us to integrate all the parts of ourselves (conscious and subconscious, past and present) so that we can be aware of how our thoughts, emotions, and habitual patterns influence us. Through insight, we come to know ourselves deeply, and we strengthen our relationship with ourselves.

While insight requires that we be reflective and honest with ourselves about areas for growth, it should not be used to beat ourselves up with could-haves or should-haves. Likewise, while insight provides the opportunity to celebrate our past accomplishments and successes, it should not be used as a measuring stick against which to judge ourselves or others.

By using our insight, we are better able to understand how our life experiences, beliefs, and emotions influence the way we interpret events and impact others. When we reflect on our choices, thoughts, and split-second reactions, we begin to see how some of the "programs" installed in our subconscious minds influence us. Using insight also allows us to reflect upon and apply the lessons learned from past experiences to support our future endeavors. We learn what not to do again, and how recent successes can be leveraged to produce even more of them in the future. For example, I can reflect on a conflict I had with another person and identify the thoughts and beliefs that triggered my response and begin to heal that part of myself. I can likewise analyze a recent accomplishment to identify the steps I took to get there and see what parts of that experience I can apply to my next goal.

In educational settings, insight is crucial for disrupting the impact of implicit bias and for creating more inclusive school communities. As we discussed in the first chapter, implicit biases are the attitudes or stereotypes that affect our understanding, actions, and decisions unconsciously. Through Insight (and heaps of self-compassion), we can identify the biases and judgments we have about ourselves and others. Just this act of acknowledgment supports us to take a profound step towards removing those beliefs and mitigating the influence they have on our subconscious reactions. When we do this kind of self-work, we deepen our relationship with ourselves and build our self-love. We also automatically begin to shift how we interact with our students and colleagues.

Looking Back

In the last chapter, we gave our intellectual sides a big party by diving into the basics of education change management! We discussed how creating change requires a thoughtful plan as well as supportive conditions for carrying out that plan. In that discussion, we identified how collaboration, communication, and coordinated implementation give new policies their best shot at being a success. Next, we learned what supportive conditions need to exist for people to be most effective in the workplace. We also gained some strategies for how to create the conditions for meaningful collaboration.

In my personal reflection, I discussed how life events forced me out of the comfortable (yet destructive) reliance I had on my intellect. I explained how changing three jobs in three years forced me to reflect on my life, my habitual patterns, and my choices in a new way. When we left off, I realized that the thinking I was doing was not working, but I didn't know what to do to change it.

Looking Forward

As we examine insight, we will revisit the subconscious and conscious minds, with a focus on beliefs. We'll discuss how values and beliefs are formed and influence the way we see ourselves and our opportunities. We will also talk about how our cultural identities form a core part of our beliefs and shape the way we interpret our experiences. This will include how beliefs and cultural norms play out in our classrooms, and some ways to create safer and more enriching learning experiences for our kids. Finally, drum roll please, we will discuss ways to change the beliefs we no longer want to influence us! We'll learn how to transform those unintentional "mom moments" by harnessing the power of our subconscious and conscious minds to shape the realities we want to experience.

For our exploration into Insight, we will be putting on our glasses again, but this time with colored lenses. These lenses represent the influence that our subconscious beliefs and programming have on how we see the world. They color every experience and interaction we have—they are how we look at the world.

Why Insight?

Insight is the practice of introspection, coupled with compassion and mindfulness. We can define **mindfulness** as being in the present moment; we're in the here and now rather than lost in thought about past or future events. Through insight, we connect with our thoughts and feelings so that we can identify habitual patterns and unearth limiting beliefs that prevent us from living up to our potential. To do this, we must be the *Warriors of the Human Spirit* that Margaret Wheatley encourages us to be when she says, "[warriors] learn to see clearly into the nature of situations and practice to cultivate our own wakefulness with enthusiastic perseverance" (2018). Taking honest stock of our thoughts and beliefs is nothing short of warrior work. It takes bravery, determination, and an unshakeable faith that cultivating our wakefulness will make a difference. It also requires an incredible amount of love, for ourselves and others. When we recognize that each of us is moving through the world with a unique pair of lenses that shape how we show up and experience reality, then it allows us to drop some of our judgments and be more accepting of others. Pretty cool, right?

Another Peak Under the Hood

In *What's Self-Love Got to do With It*, we discussed how the subconscious and conscious minds work together to create our realities. In that, we unveiled three big ideas:

> **Big Idea #1:** We have both subconscious and conscious minds that work together to shape our experiences and sense of self. Most of the time, it is our subconscious minds that are in control, reacting to stimuli based on past programming.

> **Big Idea #2:** Our subconscious minds make associations and decisions based on our prior knowledge, often without our conscious awareness.

Big Idea #3: Our subconscious minds hold implicit biases that we may not consciously agree with but that nonetheless influence how we view and treat ourselves and others.

What we haven't gotten to yet is the connection between our beliefs and our conscious and subconscious minds. Getting a handle on our beliefs lays at the heart of Insight because beliefs are closely entwined with how we understand and move through the world. By using our insight, we can begin to see the difference between limiting beliefs (ones that hold us back) and empowering beliefs (ones that allow us to realize our dreams). When we can do that, we can change the programming in our subconscious minds and thus our overall outlook. We change the tinting on our lenses.

What Are Beliefs Anyway?

Before we jump into more of the origins and impact of beliefs, let's further define them. First, we'll clarify the difference between values and beliefs as they are often paired together. Secondly, we'll discuss the various components of beliefs. **Beliefs** are ideas, perceptions, or emotions that we hold to be true, even if we have no tangible proof of their validity. **Values** are a person's principles or standards of behavior. Our values represent deeply held beliefs and cultural norms that serve as guideposts for how we live our lives. Since values reflect our principles and cultures, we won't be seeking to change them here. Instead, we'll get much deeper into beliefs. Beliefs are where judgment of self and other can arise. They are also where we can make real shifts towards leading more empowered lives if we can identify and change the ones that are limiting or negative.

Beliefs are dynamic concepts that are informed by multiple sources of information. Dr. Andrew Newberg is a neuroscientist, and Mark Waldman is a therapist, and together they have extensively studied the origin and influence of beliefs. They say that beliefs contain four interactive components: Perception, Cognition, Social Consensus, and Emotional Value (2006).

- "Perception" represents information we take in through our senses (what we can see, hear, feel, taste and smell);
- "cognition" includes the processes our brain uses to organize and make sense of the world (such as thinking, reasoning, understanding, learning, and remembering);
- "social consensus" represents the norms and input we receive from our community of origin (this includes our smaller social circle and larger society); and
- "emotional value" establishes the intensity and value we place on our experiences (how strongly we react to our environment) (pp. 21-22).

Each of the four elements of a belief influences and shapes the others. Through those interactions, our brains make meaning about the world around us and confirm what we hold as core beliefs, including our spirituality. Each element also has what Newberg and Waldman call "volume control." This means that depending on the information the mind is processing, the extent to which each of the four elements can identify with or accept the truth of it, and the greater the overall volume, the more likely a belief will take hold (p. 22).

Newberg and Waldman use the following example to show how volume control works. Imagine a stranger has come up to you and told you that you are now a millionaire, but you only have $5 in the bank. While your emotional response may be high (the idea of having that kind of money triggers a pretty significant and positive emotional reaction), your cognitive processes (your working knowledge of the amount of money in the bank) would be even stronger. It would overrule the emotional response and effectively cause you to disbelieve the statement. Now imagine that the stranger is a lawyer and in his hand is a check for a million dollars from a long-lost wealthy relative. When you take that check to the bank, they certify that the check is valid. In this case, all four elements are aligned—you can see and touch the check (perception), you are receiving it from an authority, and the bank has validated it (social consensus), the check clears, and you can see the new balance in your bank account (cognition), and you're excited (emotion). Through this process, you would come to believe that you are a millionaire (2006, pp. 22-23). Congratulations!

This idea of volume control helps to explain how our minds evaluate and accept beliefs as truth. While in the example above, all four areas needed to come into agreement for you to believe that you are a millionaire, all four areas do not need to be onboard for us to believe in something. Social Consensus and Emotional Value can influence our Perception and Cognition and allow us to believe in things that we cannot see or process consciously. A good example of the influence of Social Consensus is a belief in God. If we grew up around people with deep religious beliefs, then the social consensus that God exists would compensate for our lack of perceptual evidence. If we augmented this social influence by developing our understanding of God through further study, then our cognitive belief would grow, which would further support our acceptance that there is a God (2006, p. 23).

The meaning or value we place on our beliefs also has a heavy influence on how strongly beliefs take hold, and this, in turn, is influenced by our emotions (2006, p. 31). According to Newberg and Waldman, our emotional responses to experiences become mapped into our brains through the limbic system, the emotional circuits of our brains, and these emotional responses help to give our lives meaning (p. 31). They say, emotions "bind our perceptions to our conscious beliefs, making whatever we are thinking about seem more real at the time…[and] strong emotions—particularly anger, fear, and passion—can radically change our perceptions of reality" (p. 32). Deeply held beliefs produce a strong emotional reaction that changes how we experience events. Conversely, if a thought or perception does not produce an emotional response, it may never reach our conscious awareness (p. 32).

To understand how emotions and beliefs influence our perception of reality, consider this example from my life. Just recently, my son and I were walking our dogs. As we were walking, my son noticed that one of our neighbor's fence posts was loose. Being nine, he was drawn right to it and was absent-mindedly pushing on it while he waited for me to catch up to him. Just as I drew close, a strange man drove up on his bicycle and scolded my son for touching the fence, telling him to be careful and to not make the broken area worse. I saw red. I glared at the man, told him to mind his own business and that my son hadn't done anything to the fence. The man sheepishly apologized and said that he was just worried that a loose nail would hurt my son. As the man biked away, my son turned to me and said, "You're becoming a grumpy old lady!"

All three of us had very different experiences of reality during that exchange. As my son and I talked about the situation, I tried to explain to him what I was feeling in that moment and he told me what he saw. I can only guess at the poor man on the bicycle's experience. As a mother, all kinds of protective instincts fired off when a strange person approached my son. I also felt judged, which triggered beliefs and worries about my parenting. Did the man think that I was an absent-minded parent who is unaware of her child's actions? Was I being too lax and allowed my son to be endangered? Who was this man to tell my son what to do? Those split-second responses caused my inner mama tiger to leap forward, and I was in attack mode.

My son, on the other hand, barely registered the situation until I reacted. He is accustomed to adults telling him what to do so he just accepted the man's feedback as a part of what it is to be a kid. He also knew that he wasn't being rough with the fence, so he had no reason to register the man's comments as particularly noteworthy. The man, I'm guessing, was trying to be helpful and didn't think about how his comments might land on me. He saw what he assessed as a dangerous situation and intervened.

After calming down with a few deep breaths and debriefing with my son, I felt sheepish. I could now see the situation from his and the bicyclist's point of view. From their standpoints, my reaction was way out of balance to the situation. The instinct to protect my son, and defensiveness about my parenting skills, caused me to experience the bicyclist's behavior as a threat. My son, who lacks both parental instincts and beliefs about parenting, remained calm and unaffected. He probably would have forgotten about the incident within a few moments had I not reacted as I did. This bicyclist will likely think twice before intervening in a situation like that again!

While experiencing strong emotions isn't always fun, they are a great source of transformation! If we want to produce dramatic shifts to how we feel day-to-day, we only need to focus on those experiences that elicit a strong emotional response because they'll be attached to deep-seeded beliefs. Want to feel more joy? Start paying attention to those moments of happiness and see what experiences produce that feeling. Want to feel less anger? Start paying attention to the situations that make you angry and decipher what beliefs are running behind the scenes. From the fence incident, I saw that I had some limiting beliefs about my failings as a parent that I needed to unpack.

This is what Insight offers us. Insight gives us the ability to reflect on our experiences and become aware of the beliefs that are shaping our reality. Insight coupled with Intellect help us to notice patterns—situations that always produce anxiety, fear, anger or joy—so we can learn from them. Once we have some powerful emotional responses to unpack, they also support us to understand how perception, cognition and social consensus are contributing to our overall experience.

Big Idea #11:

Perception, Cognition, Social Consensus, and Emotional Value affect how we form beliefs and how closely with identify with them. The stronger our emotional response to a belief, the more deeply it is held in our minds.

Make it Yours:

Select a belief that you hold to be true, such as, *The Universe Has My Back.* Try to break it down into the four elements:

- Perception: What physical evidence do you have about it?
- Cognition: How do you make meaning about this belief?
- Social Consensus: How is this belief reflective of the values and norms of your family, culture, or larger society?
- Emotional Value: How strongly do you relate to this belief? What reaction is elicited if someone disagrees with it or holds an opposing belief?

Where Do Beliefs Come from?

Now that we understand the core elements of beliefs, let's take a look at how many of them are formed. Hint: This is where we get all those buttons that get pushed! It's also where we get a lot of our greatest strengths and our sense of identity. This is where the shading on our lenses comes from.

We form our beliefs and sense of self in distinct stages that coincide with our brains' development. Through his study of brain waves, Dr. Bruce Lipton has found that during each stage, the level of consciousness we are in affects how our brains take in and store information (Lipton, 2012a). These levels of consciousness move from a hypnotic-like state where we store as much information as possible to one where we exert more discernment over the information we take in. Through the course of our development from infants to adults, this information processing forms our self-identity, our values, and our core beliefs. Figure two demonstrates those stages, with our subconscious development represented by the darker shape.

Figure 2: Stages of Subconscious and Conscious Development

 Stage 1:

Ages 0-7

Almost all information is stored in the subconscious mind.

 Stage 2:

Ages 8-12

Conscious identity and discernment begins.

Most information continues to be stored in the subconscious mind.

 Stage 3:

Ages 13-21

Conscious identity takes precedence as youth develop independence.

Some information continues to be stored in the subconscious mind.

The first stage starts even before we are born! Beginning in utero and until age seven, young children's brains are like sponges where they absorb as much information as possible. They do this without conscious awareness or evaluation; information just gets installed right into the core processing centers of the subconscious mind (Lipton, 2010). Children take it all in— facial expressions, emotional responses, physical actions, and language.

Through observation and trial and error, kids learn the basics for physical survival (the stove is hot), as well as social norms (we wear clothes in public), and cultural values (it is disrespectful to look adults in the eyes). They also hard-wire core perceptions about themselves based on the messages they hear (I am smart, I am dumb, I am lovable, I am safe). During this stage, the goal is to learn the rules of the road, the traits that will enable them to stay a part of their immediate family and tight-knit social circle. Children primarily learn these rules by monitoring the positive or negative reactions of those around them, particularly their parents.

At around age eight and lasting until age 12, children begin to form a sense of self that is distinct from their immediate families. During this stage, children start copying others, and trying on different values and beliefs to see what "fits." While still highly suggestible, children begin to analyze and discriminate between the information they receive and what they will keep—they are no longer exclusively logging information into their subconscious minds (Lipton, 2012a). Instead, their conscious minds come online and start to ask some questions and begin to reject some of the messages they receive about themselves or the world around them. In this developing independence, kids start seeking role models from outside the home and can be heavily influenced by authority figures such as teachers, coaches, and religious leaders. Throughout this stage, kids' sense of self and their beliefs are still being formed and installed in the subconscious mind, but there is some conscious will applied as well.

Finally, between ages 13 and 21, young adults seek to establish themselves independent from their families and are most heavily influenced by their peers. In their effort to form their unique sense of self, adolescents and young adults may try to break away from the norms of their family and immediate community, consciously forming new groups with like-minded peers instead (Lipton, 2012a). During this stage, what our friends think is often more important than our parents, and we start to apply a critical eye towards the values, beliefs, and norms that we readily accepted and abided by when we were younger. For example, if a young adult grew up in a home with strict religious values, he or she may seek friends with more moderate views. In my case, as a Berkeley kid raised with few rules, my sisters and I went the other way. We've opted for social groups and careers that provide more structure and stability than what we had in our home and community.

Throughout our adult lives, we continue to add information to our subconscious minds, but we should not underestimate the impact of the learning during our early years. Because many of our beliefs and responses are programmed during the first 12 years of life when we were not actively picking or choosing them, they have a profound influence on us even if we don't consciously agree with them as adults. This is significant because Lipton says that many of the messages we internalize are negative and disempowering. Since the subconscious mind takes over when the conscious mind is not paying attention (which is 95% of the time!), we unconsciously replay those patterns, messages, and beliefs throughout our days without even being aware of it (2013, pg. 71). This is where the 3 Eyes and self-work come in to help us! With insight, we learn to identify our core programming and how it is influencing us. Through self-work, we begin to reprogram the parts that we do not want; we rewire our computers.

For example, I received messages as a kid that vulnerability was a sign of weakness. That belief is still there, running in the background and influencing how I respond to situations where I feel vulnerable. If as an eight-year-old I had a hard time crying during E.T., you can probably imagine how it has looked as an adult! If I feel backed in a corner, rather than taking a moment to identify my feelings and choose an aligned response, my instinct is to put up my armor and prepare for battle (think of the poor bicyclist).

This has also meant that during times when I have most needed love and support, I've unintentionally pushed people away. For much of my life, I wasn't aware that that belief was there—I just experienced the pain and suffering that resulted from it. With the gift of insight and quite a bit of self-work, I have been able to identify this limiting belief and am starting to rewire my learned responses to vulnerability. As a result, I am better able to catch myself before the armor is already on and the battle is underway. Instead, I can relate to the pain I am feeling and sit with it. I am even learning to ask for support! Rewiring our beliefs is a process, especially our core ones, but it is entirely possible.

Big Idea #12:

Our values, beliefs, and social norms are subconscious filters that affect the way we experience the world. They are so well-established that we don't even know they are there. Like a pair of sunglasses, they color every aspect of how we experience our lives.

Culture and Beliefs

Another element of our subconscious programming is the socialization we receive from our families and community. This extends beyond the norms and the messages we receive about our character from our immediate family (such as one the one I have about vulnerability). While those messages are a big part of our subconscious programming, we also hardwire core understandings about ourselves and others based on culture. As we discussed above, *Social Consensus* represents one of the four core elements of beliefs, and it comprises the agreed upon customs and behaviors of one's society. Another way to label "social consensus," then, is culture. Social consensus impacts us both as members of our cultural groups and as well as members of our larger society. While both have a profound impact on us, depending upon our cultural group, we are either seen as an insider or an outsider within broader society. This insider or outsider status can have an effect on our well-being and access to opportunity.

Zaretta Hammond is an educator and author who has done extensive work studying the connection between culture and the brain. Hammond likens culture to a tree to demonstrate how culture is internalized and expressed, as well as what happens when our cultural norms are not respected (2015). According to Hammond, *Surface* culture, the leaves and fruit of a tree, includes the observable elements of one's culture such as food, dress, and holidays. Hammond says that this surface level of culture does not carry a significant emotional charge, so if changes are made to these external symbols, it does not produce a significant emotional response (pp. 22-24).

The next level, *Shallow* culture, comprises the branches and trunk of the tree and includes the unspoken norms, communication styles, and social cues of a cultural group. It is at this level where our deep cultural values are evidenced and there is a strong emotional charge if our norms and values are not recognized (pp. 22-24). *Deep* culture, the roots of the tree, comprises foundational elements of our sense of self, including our unconscious assumptions, ethics, spirituality, and group norms. It is at this level where we feel grounded, where our brain is encoded with the worldview that we will carry into adulthood, and that governs how we learn new information (pp. 23-24).

According to Hammond, our culture is an innate part of the mental models, or schema, that we use to guide our behaviors as we move through the world—what I have been labeling as part of our subconscious programming. Hammond says **schema** are, "a set of conceptual scripts that guide our comprehension of the world," and when our schema does not match the conditions we find ourselves in, our brain registers it as a threat and goes into fight or flight mode (2015, p. 23).

Hammond uses the example of going to a restaurant to demonstrate how schema works. For just a moment, imagine going to your favorite restaurant. How do you order food? How are the tables and chairs arranged? What can you smell? What are the norms for social interaction? In this very moment, your subconscious mind has retrieved a series of associations and behaviors—your schema for going to your favorite restaurant. Now, imagine that you go there for your birthday, and everything has changed! The owners have a new menu and have stopped serving your favorite meal. They've also replaced the booth you and your family always sat in with a long "family style" table that you share with other patrons, and so on. How do you react? Are you angry? Disappointed? Do you stay and try it out? Leave and find somewhere else to go? Do you stand there dumbstruck, unsure of what to do? Your brain has just gone into fight, flight or freeze mode. Suddenly the schema you had for this restaurant does not fit with reality, and your brain registers this dissonance as a threat and prepares your body for self-preservation.

While it sounds kind of silly that our brains register changes to a favorite restaurant as a threat, it's true! They do! Why? We are hard-wired to seek experiences that minimize threats and maximize well-being, to find experiences that align with our schema (Hammond, 2015). When our schema and the circumstance we find ourselves in do not match, our brains experience it as a threat. When we detect a threat, our brains release cortisol and adrenaline and shrink our working memory as they prepare our bodies to respond to an attack. This response was essential for our early ancestors who were hunters and gatherers. Thousands of years ago, our survival depended upon our subconscious minds' ability to scan for mountain lions, for example, while we were busy collecting food. The difference between life and death hinged on our subconscious minds' ability to set our bodies into motion to protect ourselves from that mountain lion even before we consciously registered that one was stalking us.

Fast forward to today, while most of us are no longer under threat of mountain lions, our minds still go through the same process—scanning for danger and mobilizing for action. Now, our dangers are things like losing our jobs, being publicly ridiculed, or finding that our favorite restaurant has changed. Do you recall the example from chapter one about the lawn mower? How our subconscious minds aid us to safely mow the lawn while we are busy planning our outfit for a party? Yep, this is where it came from. While our needs have changed, our minds work the same way.

In classrooms, our students' sense of safety is triggered both by how they are taught and by how their teachers and peers treat them. This is especially true for our students of color and our students whose culture does not align with the dominant culture in the United States. As we have discussed, white, middle and upper-class culture predominates our social structures and media. Depending upon the cultural, gender, sexual orientation, and socioeconomic subgroups we belong to, this means that our general sense of safety and well-being may already be on alert in everyday society. Our schema does not align with what we encounter as we move through our day, see on TV, and hear from the people we meet.

This automatic response intensifies in the classroom. According to Hammond (2015), when children's cultural norms aren't recognized and included in their learning environment, their ability to learn is inhibited.

They go into fight, flight or freeze mode, their working memory shrinks, and their brains and bodies prepare for survival. This is important because as we have discussed, students of diverse cultural backgrounds are often taught by teachers that do not share their cultural background (or schema). Because of this, many of our students spend their days in survival mode and are physically incapable of learning at their full capacity.

How do we address this? One way is to train teachers in culturally responsive pedagogy. If we train teachers how to understand their students' schema and learning styles, our teachers can adapt their instructional strategies to align with their students' needs. Hammond writes extensively about this in her book. Another way is to support our educators to develop their race and cultural competence, particularly concerning implicit bias.

As we have discussed, implicit biases are attitudes or stereotypes that affect our understanding, actions, and decisions unconsciously. While I may consciously believe that everyone is equal, for example, I may have internalized messages from the media or my family that suggests that one gender, religion, sexual orientation or ethnic group is superior to others. This unconscious belief shows up when my conscious mind checks out, causing me to send subtle cues and messages that belay these biases. These internalized messages are often externalized as microaggressions.

Microaggressions are "the everyday verbal, nonverbal, and environmental slights, snubs, or insults, whether intentional or unintentional, which communicate hostile, derogatory, or negative messages to target persons based solely upon their marginalized group membership" (Sue, 2010). This means that even if I am not overtly saying racist things, I may still be unconsciously acting on and communicating bias. Microaggressions make the target person feel like they are not an accepted or welcome part of society—they are somehow other or less than. Here are a few examples:

- Assuming that the female person wearing the stethoscope is the nurse rather than the doctor.

- Asking someone who is not white where they come from—suggesting that if they are not white, they are not native to the United States.
- Reacting strongly when same-sex couples express affection (like holding hands or kissing in public) when these same behaviors exhibited by heterosexual couples are accepted without comment or response.

Microaggressions can be hard to detect and are often delivered by otherwise well-intentioned people who are unaware that their words and actions are devaluing another group (Sue, 2010). Because they can be subtle, it is tempting to write microaggressions off as harmless, but research shows that they have a profound impact on the psychological well-being of the marginalized group and contribute to the inequities in our larger society, including education (Sue, 2010).

Our beliefs and cultural norms are so well-embedded that it can be difficult even to notice them. For positive beliefs, this is excellent news! Having an innate belief that we are safe or can accomplish anything is fantastic! For limiting beliefs, however, it means that we have some work to do. Through Insight, we start paying attention to our thoughts, reactions, and feelings so that we can uncover the hidden beliefs that are getting in the way of true happiness and fulfillment. With self-work, we learn to change those beliefs into ones that we like better instead. Through school-work, we develop our race and cultural competence and learn to identify when implicit biases may be influencing how we interact with our students. We also work to create inclusive and safe learning environments that support all students to be successful.

Big Idea #13:

When our cultural norms (or schema) do not align with the circumstances we find ourselves in, it produces a reaction that our brains experience as a threat, which automatically shifts us into survival mode (fight, flight or freeze).

Make It Yours:

Think of a time where your schema did not match the circumstance you found yourself in (such as when visiting a new place, starting a new job or participating in a cultural experience different from one you were familiar with).

How did you feel? How did it affect your usual thoughts, behaviors or actions?

Why Does Understanding Beliefs Matter?

As we've discussed, we develop beliefs about ourselves and others in response to what we are exposed to, and we use values, beliefs and cultural norms to help us to understand the level of connection and compatibility we have with others. Beliefs help us to feel safe, to build relationships with others, and to create guidelines that help us to make decisions. Beliefs also act as a filter through which we experience the world and can, therefore, cloud our judgment. As such, beliefs have the power to create invisible barriers that keep us isolated. They can limit what we think we can accomplish and what we understand to be true about others. Seen from this angle, beliefs are notions that must be brought to light and interrogated so that we can be conscious about how they influence our perceptions and impact others.

As individuals, without awareness of how our subconscious programming is influencing us, we are doomed to repeat patterns, behaviors, and beliefs that we did not actively choose. Lipton (2008) points out:

> "The learned behaviors and beliefs acquired from other people, such as parents, peers, and teachers, may not support the goals of our conscious mind. The biggest impediments to realizing the successes of which we dream are the limitations programmed into the subconscious. These limitations not only influence our behavior, they can also play a major role in determining our physiology and health" (139-140).

This means that we repeat what we observed or were told as children, even if we do not consciously align ourselves with that programming as adults. While some of those beliefs genuinely reflect who we are and how we want to move in the world, why would we want to live by the ones that no longer fit?

If we have aspirations for a deep and meaningful romantic partnership, for example, a good starting place is to learn more about the beliefs we have about relationships. Did we grow up in a home where our parents fought all the time, and we heard messages that romantic love was unattainable? If yes, wouldn't we want to interrupt that belief so that we can be open to love when it arrives? Did we grow up in a home where our parents had a loving relationship, and we heard affirming messages about the power of deep commitment? Wouldn't we want to dust off those beliefs and have them working for us? While beliefs can be hard to see, they do leave traces behind. Through insight, we learn how to identify those traces and follow them back to the foundational belief. For the ones we like, we reinforce them to keep them going. For the ones we dislike, we start rewiring that programming.

In the education context, understanding how beliefs play out in the classroom is crucial to creating environments where all children can learn. Classrooms are the perfect breeding ground for continuing to repeat the larger social patterns that disadvantage individuals based on racial, sexual orientation, religious, and socio-economic lines. They can also be the places where we disrupt and reverse those narratives to create spaces where all children can learn and develop to their fullest potential. Educational researcher and instructional leader Nancy Love puts it perfectly when she says,

> "Teachers have to consciously struggle against the many ways that their prejudices distort how they view and treat children in the classroom. And they need to create zero tolerance for students' racist or sexist mistreatment of each other. Truly inclusive instruction requires not just effective instructional strategies, but continuous monitoring of racist and sexist teacher-student and student-student interactions" (2002, p. 287).

As we've discussed, creating inclusive classrooms starts when we are willing to acknowledge, if even just to ourselves, that we may be harboring biases towards our students. Through insight and a commitment to learning, we begin to catch those moments where a limiting belief or bias is operating in the background. Once we see them, we can consciously choose to change how we respond, moment by moment. We similarly help our students become aware of their language and interactions with one another. With love, communication, and awareness, we help our students to build positive connections with one another.

The first step towards creating change is choosing to be aware. When we are brave enough to face the biases and beliefs that cause us to underestimate our worth, the worth of our children, or the worth of those that are different from us, then we have taken a profound step towards creating a new reality. If we choose a career where we are responsible for other people's children, not only is changing our limiting beliefs important self-work, but it is also crucial to creating a more equitable society as a whole. If you are someone who interacts with children, it is unacceptable to throw up your hands and say that it's not your fault. If you choose to raise children, teach children or coach children, then you must understand what subconscious programming may be influencing the messages and opportunities you give to those children.

Here's an example from my own life. When I was little (before adolescence), I was one of the smallest kids in my class, but with a big voice. Always very talkative, mine was the voice that carried over the others, even at a whisper. Often when adults would meet me for the first time, they would remark at my deep, scratchy voice, and on more than one occasion, they jumped back in surprise. Every time this happened, I felt humiliated. All I wanted was to blend in and to be like everyone else, but no such luck. For example, in my elementary school, every class went to chorus once a week where we learned songs to perform for our families during quarterly assemblies. While a few kids with excellent singing voices would be singled out for solos, generally all kids were invited to sing in the chorus, but not me! The music teacher asked me to mouth the words while my classmates sang because my voice was so bad and loud.

On another occasion, my friends and I were up late one night at a sleepover, talking and laughing. The mom finally came in around midnight, exasperated that we were still up, and told all of us off. Amidst her tirade, she singled me out, saying, "Megan, your voice carries so much! You need to learn to tone it down!" While a moment before I was carefree and having a great time, being called out in that way made me feel like I didn't belong. Through these kinds of interactions, I came to believe not only that my voice was unpleasant, but also that it was just too big for some spaces.

Just recently, I was playing some old home movies from my childhood for my son, and he was startled at my voice too. Like so many adults before him, he jumped back a bit and asked if that was *really* what I sounded like! Even I marveled at my voice when I heard it, but now, with more appreciation and humor. While I have come to accept my voice, I am still self-conscious about it. I never sing in public, not even karaoke at parties, and I usually mouth most of the words to "Happy Birthday." I also intentionally modify my voice when speaking, especially when I am presenting to groups. It is always at the back of my mind.

If reactions to my voice could produce such a lasting impact on me, imagine the influence that implicit bias and derogatory comments can have on a students' beliefs about themselves. Children sink or rise to our expectations. If they are regularly presented with messages that they do not fit in or that they are somehow deficient, these messages have a lifelong impact on their self-esteem and self-efficacy. Conversely, if we give children messages that they are smart, capable, and belong, they will have the confidence to dream big and to persist even when they encounter challenges.

Returning to the example about my voice, while a few adults made me self-conscious, one teacher's positive comments have also stayed with me all these years. Ms. Lew was a 5th-grade teacher at my school, and she was beautiful and elegant and cool. All the kids loved her! When she heard my voice for the first time, Ms. Lew said that she loved it and that she'd had a deep voice when she was a kid too. Her voice was still deep but coming from her it sounded smooth and sophisticated. In that small interaction, she made me feel proud and unique. I still recall our brief exchange almost 40 years later whenever I want to feel good about my voice.

Applying Intention to our Insights

We've just learned some significant information about how our values and beliefs color the way that we see and experience the world. We also learned that many of those beliefs were installed and continue to operate without our conscious awareness. Does that mean that we are stuck with the beliefs we developed as kids? Yes and no. Just as our beliefs were installed within us, we have the power to change them if we choose to. Lipton (2008) gives us some hope about the power of the conscious and subconscious minds when they work together, saying:

> "In its self-reflective capacity, the conscious mind can observe behaviors as they're being carried out. As a preprogrammed behavior is unfolding, the observing conscious mind can step in, stop the behavior, and create a new response. Thus the conscious mind offers us free will, meaning we are not victims of our programming" (2008, p. 139).

When we become consciously aware of our beliefs, we can act as an observer and notice when they rear their heads. We can then change the subconscious programming if we choose to. For example, because I am aware that I have a belief that being vulnerable is a sign of weakness, and I have a body of lived experiences that tell me when and how that belief shows up, I am learning to catch the little bugger before it takes over. I now practice giving myself a bit of love and compassion when I start feeling my armor come up. Instead of retreating or jumping into attack mode, I try to sit with my feelings and notice the thoughts I am having. Through regular practice, this limiting belief is exerting less and less power over me.

In educational settings, there is also hope. One part is creating more inclusive learning environments through the use of culturally responsive teaching practices. The other part is doing the self-work to recognize how implicit biases may be influencing how we see and treat our students. If we do these things in combination, then we are on track to creating more equitable outcomes for kids. As Nancy Love points out, "examining belief systems takes courage and conviction. It is a true measure of our 'will to educate all children,' for it is only by breaking the silence about our racism, classism, and sexism that we can begin to break their grip on our society and our schools" (2002, p. 273). If we genuinely want to create improved outcomes for our kids, we must prioritize and support discourse about race, class, and cultural bias amongst our adults. This means fostering nurturing environments for our educators where they are safe to unpack and dis-spell the limiting beliefs they may be harboring, both about themselves and their students.

Examining our beliefs takes courage, conviction, and will, but the payoff is significant. While this is not easy or foolproof, for insight to meaningfully have an impact, we must:

- make curious self-reflection a part of life
- make intentional choices about what we believe, and
- create safe spaces for communication

Making Curious Self-Reflection a Part of Life

There's no way to get around this one: To change our beliefs, we need to want to. We also need to dedicate time to this pursuit and make it a priority. If you recall from chapter one, our subconscious minds jump in the second our conscious minds aren't looking. The only way to increase the impact of our conscious minds is to live more in the moment and to become aware of what messages take over when we're "away."

I know this seems daunting, but change is possible. We will delve into the many ways that we can become more present in the next chapter, but I'll give you a spoiler here—mindfulness is the key. To get out of cyclical thinking patterns that keep us stuck where we are, we must get a handle on the beliefs that are running the show. This is also life-work. The warrior's path is one that stretches forward without a definite end, and our job is to stick with it, to keep coming back, and to be loving and patient with ourselves on the journey.

It is helpful to liken what we are doing to peeling the layers of an onion. Each new insight, each new layer of self-discovery, reveals another one below. This means that as we identify and change one limiting belief, there will be another one waiting! Yay?! While this means that we're never *done*, it also means that as we progress, we reach increasingly greater depths of meaning and clarity. As we remove those outer layers, the greater depth of meaning also leads to greater depths of feeling and connectedness to all human-, animal-, and earth-kind. As I have undertaken this work, I feel more (the highs and the lows) and my sense of peace and calm grows every day.

Peeling the layers also requires that we replace judgment with curiosity. When we are curious, we observe events from a learner's mind and remove some of the emotional charge that can get in the way of us seeing things clearly. For example, as someone who has been in education for 20+ years, I am aware that my own limiting beliefs and subconscious programming have caused harm to my peers, my students, and their families. Rather than hiding under a rock or beating myself for my past (and future) mistakes, the best I can do is to stay vigilant. By replacing self-criticism with curiosity, I can remain open to seeing my missteps without adding them to the negative soundtrack I already have running in the back of my mind. Instead, I can take responsibility for my actions (intentional or not), apologize to those I've harmed when I can, and practice radical self-love and acceptance. Some days are far easier than others, but I am living proof that while the warrior's path never ends, you do learn new skills along the journey that make the road more comfortable and even joyful. We started the book with the following poem, and here is where it comes into play—insight.

Curiosity invites Connection

I vow to be curious.
to start conversations.
to listen with intention.
to stay open.

to inquire.
to be willing to be
surprised by what I don't
yet know about another.
to let this be my practice. (Boelman, 2017)

So, I invite you to be curious. To take the risk to open yourself up to what you may have resisted acknowledging within yourself, and to lend this same openness to those around you. Try to step into a space that is less fixed. And please, send yourself regular doses of love. When we start to peel away the layers, some of what we find isn't pretty and doesn't make us feel very good. By staying curious rather than judgmental when we uncover some of that dirt, we can observe it with detachment and move towards releasing it with more ease. If we judge, on the other hand, it sends up our defense mechanisms and makes creating change more difficult.

Make Intentional Choices About What You Believe

Once we become aware of the thoughts and beliefs that are running in the back of our minds, we can begin to choose the ones we want there instead. Researchers estimate that we have between 12,000 to 70,000 thoughts per day. We are thinking machines! 98% of those thoughts are repetitive, and 80% are negative (Hawthorne, 2014). While these numbers may initially feel disheartening, it is also great news. It means that if we can change the nature of just one of our negative thoughts, the impact is exponential. Not only will we experience the one-time benefit of shifting that negative thought, but it will change the pattern of those thoughts moving forward, providing a lasting positive impact on our repeating thoughts. One layer of the onion removed.

So how do we begin to get ahold of the thoughts that are running in the background? Well, again, mindfulness is essential. We need to slow down, notice our thoughts and pay attention to what pops up. I mentioned earlier in this chapter that while beliefs are deeply embedded in our subconscious minds, they do leave traces behind. Our thoughts and feelings are those traces, little clues to the beliefs that lie at their source. To follow those traces, it takes the curiosity we discussed above. Curiosity provides a level of detachment so that we can observe our thoughts rather than be consumed by them. When we can do that, we can do as Lipton suggests, and build a partnership between our conscious and subconscious minds to change the beliefs we don't want.

With thousands of thoughts running through our heads all day, how can we possibly get a handle on them? The simple answer is that we can't! We *can,* however, capture themes and evidence of recurring beliefs. Once we can begin to see those patterns, then we can rewire our brains and align our habitual thoughts to those that we desire. This is a moment by moment practice. The first step is to become aware of a limiting thought as it is occurring. Then we follow that thought back to its source—a negative belief about ourselves or others. Over time, those repetitive thoughts and beliefs become easier to detect. Each time we do, we simply replace the self-criticism with self-care, the limiting thought with an affirming one instead. Below, we'll discuss strategies for doing just that.

Don't Gotta Catch 'em All

Stepping into the role of the observer requires that we separate our identification with our thoughts. To do this, we need to remember that our thoughts are not facts. Our thoughts are merely subconscious programming doing its thing—applying interpretations to events at split-second speed, based on prior experiences and programming. A simple activity to observe our thoughts, and that has produced profound results for me, is to jot down what we're thinking. This sounds easy enough, but our thoughts are so pervasive and rapid that it can be tricky.

My son is a huge Pokemon fan. Pokemon is a Japanese game that originated with cards, but that now also has an app that allows you to play on your phone. In Pokemon, humans try to capture various creatures (called Pokemon) by throwing Pokeballs at them. If done correctly, the creature gets sucked into the Pokeball and becomes part of the human's collection of creatures. Each creature has unique powers—Pikachu has the power of electricity, Jirachi has the power to make your wishes come true, and so on.

There are more than a hundred of these little guys. Once captured, humans befriend the Pokemon, getting to know their strengths and challenges. The humans battle with the creatures in places called gyms and try to defeat their opponents by matching their creatures' powers against their opponents'. The winner takes possession of the gym. The more a Pokemon battles, the stronger it gets. The stronger it gets, it evolves into a different, more powerful creature. For example, Charmander is a little lizard-like creature with the power of fire. He evolves into Charmeleon, which is more dinosaur-like, and eventually into Charizard, a dragon. Chamander's powers and ability to inflict damage grows along with his size and shape.

The catchphrase for Pokemon is, "Gotta catch'em all!" and your job as the player is to try to acquire as many Pokemon as possible. Excellent marketing strategy for selling the card version of the game. My son has dozens of them. On the app, these creatures appear on a GPS map that mirrors where you are walking and makes it look as though the Pokemon are on the road with you. When going on walks with my son, this means that we stop just about every five feet or so while he tries to catch creatures by throwing virtual Pokeballs with my phone. Not a fast or efficient way to go on a walk! The game *is* a lot of fun though!

Capturing Pokemon is a great way to think about capturing our thoughts. Like the Pokemon, our thoughts can be elusive, and we need to apply some attention and focus on catching them. Once we find them, they have a lot they can teach us. We can learn more about how they help us and how they get in our way, and we can trace them back to the core beliefs that are generating them. Also like Pokemon, the more repetitive the thought, the more powerful it gets. Our Charizard thoughts are those that represent our core beliefs. They have the most power for destruction (when used against us) and for our benefit (when directed towards the things we want). Finally, like Pokemon, when we capture our thoughts and beliefs, we gain control over them. We can begin to direct the ones we like to work for us (*I can do anything I put my mind to!*) and release the ones that are not serving us (*I'm so stupid!*). We can think of our self-work as doing battle in the gym. The battle, in this case, is exerting more intention over our subconscious thoughts. We can use our thoughts of self-compassion and love to neutralize the power of our self-criticisms and judgment.

Unlike Pokemon, we don't have to try to catch them all. A few thoughts will do. Just as it is crazy-making for me that a two-block walk with my son can take a half an hour, so too would it be to try to capture all of your thoughts. If you were to try to do that, you'd be at it all day, stopping every few seconds to catch another. Not realistic, efficient, or fun! Instead, you just need to try to catch a few. I have found that good times to capture my thoughts are during meetings at work (lots of downtimes there) while doing mundane chores like washing the dishes, or when I'm running.

Think of a few times during the day when you can step into the role of explorer, hunting for your Pokemon. Before you head out, gather your Pokeballs (the best place for you to take notes). This can be on a piece of paper or journal, in your phone, or on your computer. Pick the format most comfortable for you. I use a little notebook that is small enough to carry with me throughout my day. Capture your experiences in three categories: Thought, Feeling, and Emotion. Next, start exploring and catch your Pokemon! Try to think of capturing your thoughts as an epic adventure! Here are some examples of what I've captured.

Table 2: Thoughts, Feelings, and Emotions Log

Thought	Feeling	Emotion
I think I overshared. People don't like me.	Tightness in the chest	Fear and worry
I'm really glad that I have such cool people to work with.	Openness in my body, heart racing a bit	Happy
I'm so bored! How many times do I need to hear this person talk about her project?	Tightness in the chest	Annoyance

I hope that I am doing a good job with my client. Is she happy that she chose to work with me? Will she ask for her money back?	Tightness in the throat	Anxious

The goal of this activity is to capture as many of these moments as you can throughout the day, without reviewing what you write. Just capture and move along. Do this activity for three or four days in a row. This small amount of time will provide you with a wealth of information about your inner thoughts. After you have tracked your thoughts for a few days, take another day to give some distance between yourself and the events that were ruling your mind during those days. Then give yourself a big mental hug and check out what you tracked. Do you see any repeating thoughts? How did you feel most of the time? Can you detect an empowering or limiting belief at the root of your thought patterns?

Make It Yours:

You guessed it, give this activity a try! Step into your curiosity, grab your Pokeballs and catch some Pokemon.

After you've collected some thoughts, review them.

- Is there a common theme?
- How many of your thoughts are critical? Generous?
- How often do you feel happy, sad, anxious?
- Can you trace your thoughts back to a limiting or affirming belief?

When you start on this adventure, I recommend you start small—go for a Charzard. These are thoughts and beliefs that are less charged and therefore will be easier for you to observe without getting hooked.

Once you develop your ability to recognize some of the easier ones, you will be able to start capturing the ones that exert more power over your thoughts and feelings.

The first time that I did this, I was stunned by the results. As an introspective person, I *thought* that I had a good handle on what was on my mind. I was humbled to see how many of my thoughts were about my desire to be liked and accepted by my peers. Repeatedly, I saw examples of how I was second-guessing things I had said. I spent a lot of time scanning the room and trying to interpret reactions, fearful that I was going to be shut out of the group or lose my job. It was a constant theme. Aligned with those negative thoughts were tightness in my chest, constriction in my throat, fear, and anxiety.

This activity revealed a huge limiting belief that I was carrying around, that I was unlovable. Once I could see that limiting belief so clearly mapped out in my notes, it became easier for me to catch it in the moment and to start to change the narrative I was telling myself. Now, when I find myself questioning what I say in meetings, I remind myself that I am safe and that I am doing the best I can. This simple shift has done wonders for my self-esteem and sense of calm.

Listen to Your Body

While thoughts themselves provide a pathway for detecting our beliefs, our bodies and emotions also hold valuable clues. Why? Emotions set off a release of chemicals in the body that we experience as physical sensations (sweaty palms, shortness of breath, elevated heart rate, blushing, and so on). Getting in tune with the physical sensations tied to our emotions, therefore, gives us further insight into what's happening in our minds and what we are feeling. Another way to catch our Pokemon.

In addition to noting our general physical sensations, there is a growing body of research that suggests that our hearts and our guts have vital information to tell us. Authors Grant Soosalu and Markin Oka suggest in their book, *mBraining: Using Your Multiple Brains to do Cool Stuff* (2012), that humans actually have three brains, rather than just one. They cite recent research in neuroscience, showing that within our hearts and guts are neurons, similar to those that are in are head-brains. These neurons perceive and process information and communicate with the head-brain. This is not to say that we have mini-brains with the level of complexity and precision of our head-brains residing in our hearts and guts. Instead, they have some similar components to our head-brains that makes them more attuned to what is going on than we may give them credit. They are more than just blood and food processing centers, and they connect to our head-brains on a more complex level than merely to communicate about these discrete functions.

Soosalu and Oka say that each area of the body is not only responsible for their core biological functions (processing blood and food), but also for assimilating specific types of information. If we build more intentional connections between our three information centers, then we can use them to get in tune with our beliefs and to make decisions. Soosalu and Oka attribute core functions to each information center and even cite cultural norms to demonstrate that in many ways, we have long known that each part of our bodies contributes to our overall sense of well-being and empowerment.

Table 3: Head, Heart, and Gut Intelligence

Area of Body	Intelligence**	Common Expressions and Folk Wisdom*	Implications***
Head	Cognitive Perception Thinking Making Meaning	"Use your head." "Don't let emotions override your head."	Primary Role: Logical thinking; makes sense of the world and provides executive control. Highest expression: Creativity
Heart	Emoting Relational Affect Values	"Follow your heart." "Be true to your heart."	Primary Role: Seat of love and desires, goals and dreams, affection, relational issues, and moral rightness. Highest expression: Compassion

| Gut | Mobilization

Self-Preservation

Core Identity

Intuition | "Go with your gut response."

"Trust your gut." | <u>Primary Role:</u>
Manages immune function, protection, self-preservation, self-identity, and gut-felt desires.

Highest expression: Courage |

*Soosalu and Oka, 2012, pp 22
**p. 45
***pp. 46-47

According to Soosalu and Oka, when the three "brains" are not in alignment, or if one is overriding the others, we experience disharmony in our lives. Examples of this disharmony include:

- When we encounter an internal conflict between our thoughts, feelings, and actions.
- We find it difficult to make decisions.
- Something is preventing our motivation to take action.
- We sabotage ourselves from achieving our goals.
- We experience disempowering emotional states such as depression and anxiety (p. 60).

When the three information centers are aligned, on the other hand, we can marshal the effort, focus and will we need to take action towards our goals. Good times to check in with all three information centers are when we are setting goals, making decisions or trying to solve complex problems. Our three brains also aid us when we are trying to gather the motivation and courage to make a significant life change or when we want to change a habitual behavior, like quitting smoking (2012, pp 60-61).

To get a handle on whether the three information centers are in alignment, Soosalu and Oka point to both felt-experiences (sensations in the body) and emotional expressions (including positive, negative or neutral feelings). If you recall our strategy for catching Pokemon, in addition to our column for thoughts, we also noted body sensations and emotions. Depending on the physical sensation or emotional reaction we identify, this could point to either misalignment or alignment between the three information centers. If the three intelligences are not in agreement, we should pause and further assess the situation before taking action. If they are in alignment, we should proceed full steam ahead. How can we tell? They are the same sensations we've discussed before and include tightness or openness in the chest, stomach aches or butterflies, or a general feeling of calm and well-being. Emotions (and the physical symptoms they create) include fear, anger, excitement, hope, and love.

Author and spiritual teacher Zen Cryar DeBrucke has been using a strategy for tuning in to the information centers in our bodies for over two decades. DeBrucke (2016) says that each of us has an Internal Guidance System (IGS) that if tapped into, can provide us with useful information to guide our lives and choices. According to DeBrucke, your "inner GPS contains your life's specific roadmap, which shows on a soul level all the things you are here to participate in, experience, and achieve" (p. 4). DeBrucke says that our IGS guides us by giving us sensations in our bodies, in three specific areas: our throats, chests, and solar plexus.

As a thought appears in our minds, our IGS is listening, letting us know whether our thoughts are true, aligned with our life purpose, and taking us towards greater health and happiness (DeBrucke, 2016, p. 5). If we learn to feel into our bodies, especially at times when we are seeking clarification about a choice we must make, our bodies will assist us in identifying the 'right' answer. DeBrucke calls these signals as Openings and Closings. Openings and closings give us physical validation as to whether the thoughts we are having are true or false. DeBrucke describes the *opening* feeling as that of expansion, a release of pressure, and a relaxing feeling; while *closing* produces a feeling of constriction or pressure in the region of the body between the throat and the chest (pgs. 12-13).

Doctor James Doty is a neurosurgeon who also studies how meditation and compassion influence our health and well-being. He cites research that shows that the heart and brain communicate back and forth via the vagus nerve. The vagus nerve runs from our brains down our spinal cords and is responsible for communication between our throats, hearts, lungs, and abdomens and the brain (Seymour, 2017). Doty says that there are far more connections going from our hearts to our brains than the other way around and uses this information to demonstrate the power of our emotional responses to influence our thoughts. Doty says, "we separate the mind as rational, and the heart as relational, but ultimately the mind and heart are part of one unified intelligence. The neural net around the heart is an essential part of our thinking and our reasoning. Our individual happiness and our collective well-being depend on the integration and collaboration of both our minds and our hearts" (2016, p. 230-31). Learning to quiet our minds and tap into our bodies provides us with valuable information that enhances our true understanding of what we are experiencing and promotes more well-rounded decision-making.

Big Idea #14:

Our bodies are trying to communicate with us. Tapping into the sensations in our throats, chests or stomachs can give us valuable information about whether the thoughts we are having or actions we are considering taking are in our best interest.

For me, dropping out of my mind and into my body has been transformative. As a chronic overthinker, it is easy for my thoughts to hijack me, taking me down lines of thinking that detract me from where I want to be, or that throw me into repetitive (often negative) thoughts that can consume hours and days. By learning to feel into my body when triggering thoughts start to kick off, I have been able to stop some of those thoughts from taking hold, and instead, can be more present and open.

If you look back to Table Three, one of my notations was as follows:

Thought:	Physical Sensation:	Emotion:
I think I overshared. People don't like me.	Tightness in the chest	Fear and worry

As I tracked my thoughts over a series of days, I noticed that many of them centered on fears about how I communicate and about whether I talked too much or was too blunt. As you can see from the example above, when I had the thought that I had over-shared, I simultaneously felt a tightness in my chest and felt fear and worry. If we apply Soosalu, Oka, and DeBrucke's guidance to my circumstance, then my physical and emotional responses suggested that the thought I was having was not true. The tightness in my chest shows misalignment between what my head is thinking and what my heart knows to be true. If I then trace back through all the times I have worried about my communication style, it reinforces the notion that my thoughts were not true. I have never been fired for speaking my mind and haven't been shunned by my friends and colleagues. In fact, one of the most common compliments I get is how much people value my transparency and integrity, and that I don't play "games." People tend to confide in me. I have been told more than once that people drew on my example to be brave enough to speak their truth.

Since learning about the mind-body connection, I check in with my IGS daily to see if the thoughts I am having align with my physical sensations and emotions. Like the thought tracker, if I scan my body and detect a tightness in my throat, chest or stomach, I try to tune into the thoughts I am having at that moment. If I notice a negative thought pattern running, I take a deep breath and gently redirect my thoughts in a more positive direction. I likewise compare my thoughts with my body sensations. I notice the thought I am having and detect if I feel constricted or tight in my chest or throat. If I do, I take a breath and remind myself that the thought is not true. Just by doing this simple practice, I have become much better at stopping the negative thought patterns before they consume me and I feel calm and centered more often.

Create Safe Spaces for Communication

Once we begin to get a handle on our internal thoughts and feelings, then it is time to turn our attention outwards. In our previous discussion on Intellect, we reviewed the conditions that need to be in place for people to be most effective and collaborative. As a review, here are the big ideas we uncovered:

> **Big Idea #7:** Individuals need to feel emotionally safe to fully contribute to a relationship, team, or larger organizational culture.

> **Big Idea #8:** Trust is a necessary component to all relationships, both personal and professional. We build trust through our character and our competence.

> **Big Idea #9:** Love your employees through recognition, encouragement, and by providing opportunities for personal and professional growth.

A central theme running through these "Big Ideas" is that people need to feel safe to express who they really are. Safety is fostered through trusting relationships where we are honest and open, and where we seek to understand one another. To me, this is another facet of the Warrior Work that Margaret Wheatley espouses. She says, "We can change the world if we start listening to one another again. Simple, honest, human conversation. Not *mediation, negotiation, problem-solving, debate or public meetings.* Simple, truthful conversations where we have a chance to speak, we each feel heard, and we each listen well" (2017). Great insights and healing can come when we learn to listen to one another. One of the most valuable gifts we can give another is to provide them with a safe space to speak and to be heard.

To foster trust and safety, we can intentionally cultivate nurturing relationships in both our personal and professional lives. Sonia Choquette is a spiritual teacher and speaker. She says that to have the confidence to realize our goals, we must seek out Believing Eyes. *Believing Eyes* are people who cheer us on, reflect back our assets, and keep us going when times get tough. Believing Eyes can be our parents, co-workers, partners or children, anyone we trust enough to share our struggles and dreams with. These are the people who remind us how awesome we are! When we surround ourselves with people who genuinely believe in us and want us to be successful, then we believe in ourselves even more, and our goals are more attainable. (2018a, p. 14).

Conversely, if we surround ourselves by people who are negative or critical, then their discouraging thoughts can inhibit or even undermine our efforts. These people poke at the soft spots that we have been protecting since we were children, cause us to doubt ourselves, and can make achieving our goals more difficult. A significant first step as we embark on our Warrior Work, then, is to identify the Believing Eyes we have in our lives.

Don't have any Believing Eyes? That's okay! Choquette says a great way to get them is to be the Believing Eyes for others. Support those around you. Be a positive reinforcement for their dreams. Celebrate the accomplishments of your friends, family, and colleagues. Remember that there is plenty of success to go around, so rather than competing with others, look for and appreciate all that the people around you are accomplishing. You can also be Believing Eyes for people you don't know. When we identify our role models and celebrate their accomplishments, we put more good vibes out into the world, and we focus our positive attention on the attributes that we want in our own lives. Want to be more like Oprah Winfrey? Study her and appreciate those things about her that you want for yourself. When you celebrate and are the Believing Eyes for the people in your life, you start to cultivate Believing Eyes for yourself. This kind of appreciation and support is catching, and it grows exponentially. It's a like good vibes magnet.

While Believing Eyes incredibly powerful, so are open ears. Truly listening to another is one of the greatest and simplest gifts we can give, and it's free! We usually have the answers we seek within us, and what we need is a loving and patient audience to let us work things out. When we accompany our Believing Eyes with the willingness to listen, we create a nurturing space where another can share what is truly on their minds. So, as we embark on our Warrior work, we should also seek out people who will just listen. If we don't have these people around us, we may want to find a coach or therapist who can support us. The warrior's path is not one that should be taken alone, so as you embark on your self-work, find some traveling companions.

In our school-work, listening requires that we value the perspectives of our students and families and that we make a genuine effort to understand what is important to them. Teacher, educational leader, and author Shane Safir says the key to creating more inclusive classrooms and schools is through learning to listen. Safir says,

> "Listening educators see the human experience as a complex text with listening as a form of close reading. They understand that every great lesson plan, parent conference, and teacher collaboration starts with a simple yet underutilized skill: listening. This is brave work that may not be rewarded in your evaluation, but it will exponentially increase your impact and set you apart as an educator" (2014).

To do this, Safir says that four things must be in place: (1) the willingness to slow down; (2) genuine curiosity; (3) attention to non-verbal cues; and (4) self-awareness and empathy (2014). While we may feel the urgency for change in our educational settings, for example, taking the time to listen well allows us to build connections with students and families so that everyone can come along in the change process. Lisa Delpit recommends a similar strategy. Not only is listening important, but Delpit (2018) suggests that we intentionally create spaces for parents of color to be actively engaged in determining the kind of instruction that is in their children's the best interests.

Implications

Throughout this chapter, we have explored the power of Insight. We've examined why developing our insight is essential to uncovering the subconscious programs that color how we experience our lives. Through insight, we understand ourselves on a much deeper level, allowing us to make friends with ourselves, both with the parts that we like and with the parts that we want to change. Insight also provides a bridge to connect with others, which can lead to deeper and more meaningful relationships.

Self-Work:

By learning where our beliefs come from, we can identify how they show up in our lives. We are then empowered to make different choices than the automatic ones programmed into our subconscious minds. Our thoughts, physical sensations, and emotions provide us with clues to detect our beliefs.

By embarking on the Warrior's path of introspection and intentionality, we open our awareness to new possibilities and ways of being in all parts of our lives. As our awareness deepens, the people and circumstances around us also start to change, reflecting our new level of consciousness.

School-Work:

As we begin to know and care for ourselves on a deeper level, we can face the parts of ourselves that we are not so proud of. In educational settings, it is especially vital for us to identify how implicit bias may be causing us to limit our students' potential. To counteract the power of implicit bias, we need to recognize it is there and enter into conversations with people we trust to learn a new way of being.

Our cultural identity is a powerful part of our belief system, and when our culture is not recognized or is disrespected, it sends our bodies and minds into a fight-or-flight response. For students, this response inhibits their ability to learn. We can actively work to create more inclusive and culturally-responsive settings for our students and families so that all students can learn at their fullest potential.

Discovering My Lenses

When we left on in my personal story, I had experienced three job transitions in three years. Through that experience, I was able to see how my habitual thoughts and patterns were causing me harm. While I was able to step outside of myself to be able to see this, I had no idea what to do about it. The person who I wanted to talk to about this pattern was my dad. Since he had passed away many years before, I didn't know who I could turn to for support.

Taking a Glimpse Behind the Veil

Realizing that I didn't have my father to speak to caused me to feel incredibly helpless and lost. In every family, we have our roles. Mine, basically since birth, was to be self-sufficient. I am in the middle of three girls, and the needs of my older and younger sisters always seemed to overshadow mine. The way to get my needs met and to receive praise was through self-sufficiency and strength—that's what made me stand out. That is why, while I was married and had friends and family to speak to at this acute moment of need, I could not manage to lower my defenses enough to ask for support. My dad was the one person who could always see through my façade, and I needed him now.

So deep was my need to connect with my father that I even daydreamed about going to a psychic. At that time, my schema for psychics were TV personalities like John Edward or Theresa Caputo (the Long Island Medium), or the stereotypical storefront psychic, with the neon sign of a crystal ball, wearing shawls and beads, speaking in a spooky voice. I imagined Whoopie Goldberg in "Ghost" and Professor Trelawney in Harry Potter, playing on my emotions and talking in generalities. No way was I going to someone like that! So, I figured I was out of luck. Nonetheless made a silent wish that I could find a way to connect with my dad and did my best to move on with my life. I started back with a new job in my old district and tried to regain my self-confidence.

I was utterly shocked then, when not two weeks after making my silent wish, it was answered! The universe is so cool! One night I was having dinner with an old friend when out of the blue, she mentioned that another friend of ours was seeing an intuitive coach. Our friend Sharon was a professional educator like me, and I had a great deal of respect for her. She was also not the type to be snowed over by a fake. With nothing to lose, I reached out to Sharon and asked about her experiences. She told me that she had been seeing this person for years and that through their work together, she had gained insights that had a profound impact on her life. From what I heard, this coach used her intuition to access information that supported Sharon to understand her life on a deeper level; to encourage her to identify and clear out old patterns that no longer served her. Still not sure what intuitive coaching was but trusting Sharon's experiences, I scheduled my first appointment.

When I arrived at Julie's office, I was relieved to see no evidence of crystal balls or neon signs. Julie looked like someone I would encounter at my local coffee shop—no extraordinary use of shawls or beads! She merely sat across from me and asked what I hoped for out of our session. With a lump in my throat, I laid all of what had happened over the previous three years, how lost I felt, and how desperately I wished I could talk with my dad. And so we began. Julie used her intuition (quieting her mind and opening up to the information that comes from the silence) to access insights I was unable to see on my own. Through those insights and some well-placed questions and encouragement, we slowly started to uncover the beliefs that had been getting in my way. We also identified some strategies I could use to reverse them. Those strategies included learning to connect with my own intuition through meditation, learning to let go, and trusting that a greater power than me had things under control.

These were huge steps for someone as head-centered as me! Through my intellect alone, all I had been able to do was replay the immediate issues at hand. My thinking revolved around solving those issues, but I was limited to the approaches I had used in the past. I was also unknowingly operating with a unique pair of lenses that were limiting my full understanding of my circumstances (and therefore the best way to move through them). The insights and access to my intuition that I started to develop with Julie helped me to let go of just a smidge of control. With that release, I was able to step back to see new possibilities for who I was, how I moved through the world, and what my future could be. Julie was also able to connect me with the essence of my dad that still resided within me. He was with me all along, and through Julie's support, I was able to reconnect with the wisdom and support I always gained from him.

Now What?!

Following my sessions with Julie, it was as if a ten-ton weight was lifted from my chest. I could breathe again, and I felt a kind of peace and calm that I had never known before. If the trajectory of my life was a billiard ball, moving forward in a straight line propelled by the momentum of my experiences up to that point, meeting Julie was like having that ball hit by another; while it still moved forward, the direction was changed permanently. Something had shifted in me that would never be the same again.

After seeing Julie for a while, I began yearning for a way to connect with this energy on my own. I asked Julie for some good places to start, and she referred me to books by metaphysical teachers on the Law of Attraction, beliefs, and spirituality. Each new book I read lead to a deeper level of meaning, opening more doors into the nature of the human mind and ways that we can connect with knowledge that cannot be found through our intellect alone.

I came to understand that the world I had built for myself, grounded in the belief that if only I worked hard enough, I could control my future, was wrong. I also came to understand that there are forces far more powerful than me at play and that my job is to open to love instead of hate, replace effort for stillness, self-abuse for self-compassion. A switch had been turned on that helped me to step outside of my habitual thoughts and instead connect to love, compassion, and energy of all kind (human, animal, nature, spirit). My challenge was, however, that I did not know how to reconcile this new understanding with the life I had created for myself.

Dr. Paul Kalanithi, an accomplished neurosurgeon who was diagnosed with stage four cancer in his 30's, describes this "switch" in elegant terms. As he faced his mortality, his priorities and understanding about life began to transform. He began to see that the scientific precepts upon which he had based so much of his trust and reliance could not support him as he grappled with his impending death. He says,

> "The paradox is that scientific methodology is the product of human hands and thus cannot reach some permanent truth. We build scientific theories to organize and manipulate the world, to reduce phenomena into manageable units. Science is based on reproducibility and manufactured objectivity. As strong as that makes its ability to generate claims about matter and energy, it also makes scientific knowledge inapplicable to the existential, visceral nature of human life, which is unique and subjective and unpredictable. Science may provide the most useful way to organize empirical, reproducible data, but its power to do so is predicated on its inability to grasp the most central aspects of human life: hope, fear, love, hate, beauty, envy, honor, weakness, striving, suffering, virtue.
>
> Between these core passions and scientific theory, there will always be a gap. No system of thought can contain the fullness of human experience. The realm of metaphysics remains the province [for this kind of] revelation" (p. 168-170).

The tension Dr. Kalanithi describes here is between the concrete world of facts, figures and material objects, and that of the spiritual and emotional aspects of ourselves that cannot be so easily contained or measured. Up until his cancer diagnosis, Dr. Kalanithi had rested his faith in science and in his ability to use his skills as a surgeon and scientist to define his boundaries and that of his patients. Once faced with death, Dr. Kalanithi found that science alone could not provide the depth of meaning or the answers he sought to make sense of the turn his life had taken.

Like Dr. Kalanithi, I realized that trying to confine my life and experiences to those that I could sort out in my head was not enough. Thankfully, my existential crisis came not with a terminal diagnosis, but instead, with the change of my third job in three years. Through the job losses, I was finally able to step outside of the drama I was playing in my mind to see how destructive I was being to myself. Through my experiences with Julie and my development since, I have begun forging a new path forward that is grounded in love, compassion, and mindfulness.

It is a path that started with loving myself. I now know that the fullest experience and expression of my life cannot be confined to my intellect alone. By dropping out of my head and into my heart, and by learning how to trust people and forces outside of myself, my life is becoming more vibrant and more meaningful. I am also on a journey. While the trajectory of my life changed when I met Julie, I am still who I have been, and learning to integrate my insight and intuition is the Warrior's path that I will be on for the rest of my life. I am so grateful!

Intuition

"The intuitive mind is a sacred gift and the rational mind is a faithful servant. We have created a society that honors the servant and has forgotten the gift." - *Albert Einstein*

"I feel there are two people inside me — me and my intuition. If I go along against her, she'll screw me every time, and if I follow her, we get along quite nicely." - *Kim Basinger*

Benefits of Using Intuition

We can define **Intuition** as knowing something based on instinct or feeling, rather than from conscious reasoning (Google, 2017). Intuition is quiet and subtle and is the space of calm knowing that many of us have experienced at one time or another in our lives. Perhaps it was when you met your soulmate, and you just knew they were the one. Or when you knew (without being able to explain why) that a decision you made was the right one; you could just feel it in your body, and there was no doubt or hesitation. Or when information came to you right when you needed it, but you didn't know where it came from or how you knew it, you just did.

When we're using our intuition, we tap into sources of information that cannot be arrived at through our intellect alone. Film director David Lynch says that "Intuition is the key to everything, in painting, filmmaking, business - everything...If you can sharpen your intuition, which they say is emotion and intellect joining together, then a knowingness occurs." I like what David Lynch says here, that intuition is the coming together of intellect and emotion, and I'd add imagination to the mix. When intellect, emotion, and imagination come together, we can conceive of ideas that are new and different. We can envision lives we have yet to experience and can access knowledge that lies quietly beneath the surface of our bustling minds.

Mindfulness is the gateway to our intuition. **Mindfulness** means being aware of our thoughts, feelings and body sensations in the present moment. Through practicing mindfulness, we drop into our bodies more. When we get off the hamster wheel of our minds, we're able to observe our thoughts from an objective point of view. Through mindfulness, we are more integrated, calm, and centered, and thus we are able to access the intuitive knowingness that David Lynch describes.

Looking Back

As we have progressed through this book, we have been moving from the concrete to the more etheric. In Intellect, we discussed research-based best practices for creating change in education settings. In Insight, we learned about how our thoughts and beliefs affect how we experience the world. We also dipped into the notion that we can analyze and change that viewpoint if we wish.

Looking Forward

Now, we are onto Intuition, the least tangible and perhaps the most personal of the three. It is also the creative space in which the other two lenses can be integrated and transformed to produce powerful outcomes. I'm excited to share this final lens with you because it is the last ingredient in the special sauce that can change your life!

In this chapter, we'll tap into the benefits of accessing our intuition. We'll also introduce several mindfulness strategies to make accessing our intuition easier to do. Finally, we will look at practical applications for using our intuition, and why the use of our intuition is a powerful tool for transforming our lives and our educational settings.

In my personal story, I'll share how I came to understand that the 3 Eyes are where it's at, and how integrating my intellect, insight, and intuition has enhanced my overall sense of well-being and my experiences at work. I'll end with some reflections on how my life has changed since starting on the journey I describe in this book.

It's time to put on our final pair of glasses, this time with wings on them. These fancy glasses represent the way that life can feel more rich, meaningful, and joyful when moving through the world connected to our intuition.

Intuition, Really??

Using our intuition is not a conventional practice in the United States, and therefore many of us need to learn how to use it. For me, while I naturally lean into my intellect to solve problems, I have had to make a conscious decision to learn how to detect and use my intuition. Further, while a lot of business leaders and visionaries talk about the value of using their intuition (Steve Jobs and Albert Einstein among them), we seem to be more tentative about using it in Education. Based on my observations, it seems the high-stakes expectations around making academic gains for students has made the practice of using our intuition less prevalent. Educators are also part of the system that prioritizes left-brain intellectual knowledge over right-brain imaginative and intuitive understanding. We like observable data and concrete outcomes that we can measure. It makes sense that educators can find it difficult to see how intuition fits into their work.

I actually think this is a good thing, for now. Many of us may not be ready to go on intuition alone. Because it can be difficult to decipher if the information we are receiving is coming from our intuition, or instead from implicit bias, cultural norms, or other subconscious programming, getting familiar with how to identify our intuition is essential. In educational contexts in particular, the stakes are just too high for educators to follow their "guts" without integrating other sources of information. Rather, the best opportunity we have for creating equitable outcomes for our kids is to learn how to incorporate the knowledge we gain from all 3 Eyes. For our personal development, this is also true. When we use all three lenses, the decisions we make are clearer, more balanced, and aligned with our goals.

I am not suggesting that it is impossible to tap into one's intuition instantly and accurately. Some people have an innate ability to do just that, and secretly, I'm a bit jealous of them! Because each of us needs to find our own way to tap into our intuition, we're going to spend most of our time in this chapter on strategies that will make accessing intuitive information more accessible and natural. I also want to stress that while I believe that use of our intuition is vital for being grounded and integrated educators, I respect the separation of church and state that we have in our public education settings. The content provided here is not an attempt to breach that divide, but rather, a way to allow us to access the inherent wisdom we already have within us.

Just What *Is* Intuition?

First of all, our intuitions are so cool! Learning to access our intuition is also a lot more natural, and a lot less woo-woo, than many of us may think. Connecting with our intuition is also a very personal experience. As such, it's helpful to understand intuition as being on a spectrum, based upon our beliefs. These beliefs may be influenced by past experiences, cultural norms, religious affiliations, and more. On one end, intuition can be understood as a reflection of our subconscious minds, but on the other end, intuition is information that we receive from our higher self in connection with Source (God, the Universe, collective consciousness). Below I will offer two different ways to understand intuition that range at both ends of that spectrum.

Figure 3: Spectrum of Intuition

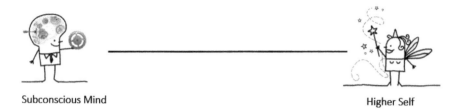

Subconscious Mind   Higher Self

Intuition as Subconscious Thoughts

Economist Daniel Kahneman sources our intuition to the automatic and immediate thoughts and ideas that are generated in our subconscious minds, which he dubs System 1. Kahneman says:

> "[System 1] offers a tacit interpretation of what happens to you and around you, linking the present with the recent past and with expectations about the near future. It contains a model of the world that instantly evaluates events as normal or surprising. It is the source of your rapid and often precise intuitive judgments" (2011, p. 58).

Kahneman posits that what we may identify as intuition is actually our subconscious minds assessing the situation we are in and drawing upon our stored memories, associations, and beliefs to make informed decisions. Because this thinking is happening so quickly, and without our conscious knowledge, the information and instincts we eventually become consciously aware of are attributed to "intuition." In actuality, it is our System 1 minds in action.

Have you suddenly known the answer to a challenge you've been facing and you don't know where you got it from? Kahneman would say that you already had that information stored in your subconscious mind, having picked up and saved it somewhere along your journey. When you needed it, your System 1 mind brought it forward. Have you walked into a room and sensed that there had just been an argument between the two folks that are in there? It is your subconscious mind again, picking up on subtle cues in the facial expressions and actions of the people who were arguing that tips you off that there had been a fight.

One of the main ideas in Kahneman's book, *Thinking, Fast and Slow*, is that we need to understand the roles of System 1 and System 2. He encourages us to know the triggers that influence each system's functionality, and how the two interact with one another. He also cautions us to be aware of the "tricks" our minds can play on us and to know just how profound the influence of System 1 can be. If we can do that, then we can make more intentional choices and check the intuitive hits we get from System 1 to ensure that the information it is providing us is reliable.

One of the places we need to apply special attention is to the influence that emotions have on our beliefs and intuitive abilities. To demonstrate the sway that emotions can have on System 1, Kahneman cites research where subjects were asked to make a split-second decision as to whether or not there were solutions to a series of word association problems. The subjects were not given enough time to solve the problems, and therefore they had to give an immediate yes or no, whichever came to mind when presented with the problem. The study found that the subjects who were in a good mood and thinking happy thoughts doubled their intuitive accuracy over subjects who were not in a happy mood. Unhappy subjects were incapable of performing the intuitive task. Their answers were completely random (2011, pgs.68- 69). Kahneman concludes that mood, "affects the operation of System 1: when we are uncomfortable and unhappy, we lose touch with our intuition" (p. 69). He also cautions, however, that "a happy mood loosens the control of System 2 (our conscious minds) over performance: when in a good mood, people become more intuitive and creative, but also less vigilant and more prone to logical errors" (p. 69).

This heightened energy state can produce overconfidence and overreliance on our intuitions, so we should "check" our decisions before proceeding, especially when the stakes are high. Kahneman suggests the way to block the errors that originate in System 1 is to, "recognize the signs that you are in a cognitive minefield, slow down, and ask for reinforcement from System 2" (2011, p.417). Here, Kahneman supports a fundamental premise of this book, that reflection and awareness of our beliefs and programming (through Intellect and Insight) are essential to clear decision-making. I call those minefields limiting beliefs and programming, and we can use our conscious minds (Kahneman's System 2) to understand and evaluate the accuracy of those thoughts. When we're able to have the two minds work together, we are better able to access information that is reliable and supportive.

> **Big Idea #15:**
>
> Emotion plays a powerful role in our ability to access intuitive information. When we are in a happy and positive mood, we are better able to access our intuition. When we are in a bad or negative mood, we lose touch with our intuitive abilities.

Intuition as Higher Self and Source

On the other end of the spectrum, spiritual teacher Sonia Choquette says that intuition is the guiding voice of our souls and is a natural and important part of who we are (2018b). According to Choquette, picking up intuitive information is as simple as being open to receiving guidance. Expect that the guidance will show up, trust your intuitive feelings when you get them, and act on your intuitive impulses (2018b, p. 2). To access our intuition, Choquette encourages us to be present in the moment and to pay close attention to the world around us. In simple words, she is asking us to be mindful. She says that "true intuition is the consequence of clear and accurate observations of the here and now. Such observations, once turned over to your subconscious mind, will lead to the most advanced and brilliant insights; and help you create healing, balance, peace of mind and a happy heart" (2018b, p. 2).

Just how do we improve our mindfulness? Choquette encourages us to develop a meditation practice. Through meditation, we learn to slow down our thoughts and to be in the present moment. *Meditation* could mean many things, and not necessarily sitting cross-legged in a room listening to recordings of babbling brooks, but it could be just that! Through regular meditation practice, it becomes easier and easier to be present with the here and now. When we can do that, we are able to pick up on the subtle intuitive clues that are all around us. In addition to meditation, Choquette encourages us to find ways to connect back to ourselves and our environment throughout the day. Connecting back could be anything from a 20-minute break for self-care to taking a walk with someone we care about, to looking out the window, or just taking a moment to appreciate nature. The goal is to take intentional breaks from the bustle of our days and our minds and to touch back in with our true selves (2018b).

Another important way to touch back in with our selves is through connecting with our hearts and emotions. According to Choquette, "we find our inner voice, and the path to personal joy in the heart. It brings our attention to the unseen subtle aspects of life and directs us toward a more creative, more loving, more healing approach to life's difficulties" (2018b, p. 7). Listening to our hearts is as simple as paying attention to how we are feeling in any given moment. When we turn our attention inwards, we can detect what we are truly thinking and feeling. Choquette says, "only when you listen with both head and heart and listen to what you feel to be honest and true will you have a clear and complete sense of real direction in life" (2018b, p. 7).

Like Kahneman, Choquette also reinforces the 3 Eyes framework. When we learn how to connect our head-knowing (Intellect) with our heart-knowing (Insight) and turn our attention inwards (Intuition), we are able to access the truth that already exists within us. Choquette also encourages us to have fun with our intuition and to explore it with an attitude of imagination and wonder (2018b, p. 24). I agree! When we explore our intuition with an attitude of wonder, it allows our hearts to remain open and playful and lets our imagination explore the unseen world of intuition and spirituality with fresh eyes.

Big Idea #16:

To access our intuition, we must be in the present moment. Mindfulness supports us to be in the present and therefore aware of our thoughts, feelings, and the subtle information that intuition provides.

Common Threads

Wherever in the spectrum that is right for you, intuition provides the opportunity to align our intellect and insight with a deeper source of knowledge that can give us a 3-Dimensional perspective. While stated in different ways, both Kahneman and Choquette encourage a partnership between the conscious and subconscious minds so that our thoughts and beliefs are aligned in the same direction. Both also stress the influence of emotions on our outlook and demonstrate that when we are in a positive and happy mood, we are better able to access our intuitive knowledge.

Make it Yours:

What is your current relationship with your intuition?

- Can you identify your intuitive impulses? Do you follow them?
- Do you feel unable to detect your intuition or distrust it?

Wherever you are in your relationship with your intuition now, how would you like for it to change? Do you want to strengthen your ability to detect it? Your ability to follow it?

Jot down a goal you have for using your intuition.

Mindfulness Matters!

We've finally arrived at mindfulness! Throughout our discussion so far, I have been pointing to mindfulness as an essential aspect of personal transformation. Let's see what all the fuss is about. Mindfulness can be defined as being aware of our thoughts, feelings, body sensations, and environment in the present moment. We are not preoccupied with past experiences or anticipating future events. We are here and now. Stanford Graduate School of Business lecturer Leah Weiss says that mindfulness is heart-mind training that can and should be used throughout the day, from home to work and everywhere in between (2018). Weiss encourages us to think of mindfulness, not as an event that occurs on a meditation cushion, but rather, as a practice for getting to know our minds and our hearts on the spot. Weiss says, "when it is done right, [mindfulness] allows us to get to know the places where our mind 'goes' and over time, to get better at putting it (gently) where we want it to be. We come to know what our heart really wants, and we improve our ability to listen to it" (2018, p. 5).

When we are in the present moment, we can consciously step back and observe the stories that are running in our minds and detect how our bodies are communicating with us. Rather than being lost in thought replaying a past event, anticipating a future event or reacting to our experiences based on old patterns and beliefs, mindfulness gives us some space. Victor Frankel was a neurologist, psychiatrist, and Holocaust survivor. His work focused on human beings' desire to have lives grounded in meaning and purpose. Steven Covey, the author of *The 7 Habits of Highly Effect People*, attributes the following concept to Frankel; "Between stimulus and response, there is a space. In that space is our power to choose our response. In our response lies our growth and our freedom."

Mindfulness supports us to take advantage of the space between stimulus and response and gain freedom from our subconscious programming. In the space of even just one breath, we can catch ourselves and make a different choice. We can check in on the story we're telling ourselves and identify if assumptions or beliefs are guiding our reactions. We can pause and scan our bodies for sensations in our throats, hearts, or guts that may reveal a truth that our heads cannot access. If we've come to know ourselves more deeply through Insight, we can check in and see if we are re-enacting habitual responses that have not served us in the past. While this sounds like a lot to consider, all of this introspection can happen in the space of one breath. We can change the course of lives and relationships through these moment-by-moment choices. Over time, with a regular mindfulness practice, that space actually feels so much longer than the time it takes to draw one breath.

Let's consider a typical scenario in my life—worrying about an upcoming meeting and the people who will be participating in it. Perhaps my thoughts are preoccupied with all that could go wrong and what I can do to make it better. How can I structure the meeting to get my needs met? How do I ensure that this time, we get to the answers I need to do my work? When I check in with my body, I notice that my throat is tight and my fists are clenched. This tells me that I am tense and that the thoughts I am having are not true. If I can release some of that tension and breathe into the openness of the present moment, I experience immediate relief and increased calm. I can also let go of some of the narrative (which is that the meeting will not go well) and see that the tension I'm building will not support me to show up as my best self in that meeting.

Perhaps I'm also fixating on someone I know will be in that meeting, who in the past has been difficult or combative. If I can notice those thoughts, I can choose a different reaction, both as I prepare for the meeting and in the meeting itself. For example, I can choose to take a breath before responding to this person's questions, or I can write out a statement I can say to myself that allows me to finish the meeting without getting pulled off-course. When I'm a participant in those kinds of meetings, I try to capture my experience—the Pokeman thought exercise we discussed in the previous chapter. If I am leading those meetings, then I set an intention before the meeting of how I want to show up and remind myself as often as I can during the meeting to stay true to those goals. For example, if my goal is to be professional, calm, and collaborative, if someone tries to pull me into their drama, I mentally remind myself that getting into a power struggle won't serve me. This alone has helped a lot! The more I practice mindfulness, the greater my ability to take advantage of the space between the stimulus and my response.

Mindfulness is also being proven to play a role in reversing the impact of implicit bias. The Kirwan Institute for the Study of Race and Ethnicity releases an annual review of research on implicit bias. In these reviews, mindfulness strategies continue to emerge as promising practices for reversing implicit bias and for increasing positive emotions between racial groups (Staats et al., 2016). Several research studies now show that mindfulness meditation decreases the influence of implicit bias by:

- changing the structures of the brain to reduce prejudice (rewiring our subconscious programming and associative responses);
- raising awareness of our biased thoughts so we can mitigate their effects (bringing our conscious minds online so we can take advantage of the space between stimulus and response);
- reducing stress (and the physical and emotional reactions stress causes); and
- fostering empathy, compassion, and communication (the self-work and school-work we've been discussing) (Staats et al., 2017, p. 45).

This research has profound implications for our educational settings. By supporting our teachers and leaders to participate in mindfulness practices, not only will they feel better overall, but they will be better able to detect and interrupt implicit biases. Biases that would otherwise cloud their judgment and influence how they treat their students.

Ready to get more mindful? The most basic form of mindfulness is just to breathe and to return oneself to the present moment. Below are examples of 12 additional mindfulness-boosting practices—what they are and a bit of what the research says about them. There is no "right" way; if you gravitate to one, try it out!

Body Scan:

When we scan our bodies, we are bringing an intentional focus back to the sensations within our bodies. While there are various ways to do a body scan, including guided meditations that support exploration from the tips of our toes to the tops of our heads, here we'll focus on simple breathing techniques. Regardless of the method, the primary goal is to connect our minds and bodies into one again.

It is easy for our thinking (intellect-based) minds to become so preoccupied that we forget that our bodies are even there! This is especially true when we become absorbed by our thoughts, are exploring the internet, or are at work. Through intentionally building the mind-body connection, we touch back in with the sensations that exist in our bodies, such as tightness in the chest or tension in our shoulders. As we've discussed, physical sensations can give us a clue to the thoughts and emotions that we are experiencing—whether we are conscious of them or not. When we touch back in with our bodies, we connect again with the wisdom and information we hold there.

Another benefit of supporting this mind-body connection is bringing our attention back on the wonder of life. Through taking even just a few deep breaths, we can touch back into the gift of having a body, which in turn helps us to appreciate all of the life that is within and around us. Buddhist monk and spiritual leader Thich Nhat Hanh suggests that as we take deep breaths we repeat the phrase, "Breathing in, I know I have a body, and my body is a wonder of life" (Hahn, 2017, p. 82). He says that this is a concrete way to enjoy having a body.

If, as we're breathing in, we notice tension, the body scan also provides us with the opportunity to release that tension and to settle into more calmness. Hanh suggests using the phrase, "Breathing in I am aware of my body and the tension in my body, breathing out I release the tension in my body," as a way to relax (p. 82). Taking a few intentional breaths while consciously calming parts of our bodies is an excellent on-the-spot way to assess our feelings, calm our minds, and ground ourselves. I practice taking mindful breaths often, including just before walking into a meeting or during a stressful conversation. Likewise, if I notice that parts of my body are tensing, I breathe in to relax those areas while simultaneously getting a gauge on the thoughts and feelings that are triggering that response.

Decluttering

Decluttering is as basic as it sounds. Simply put, decluttering means that we remove the excess clutter (material objects) that surround us so we can create spaces that are more organized and free of distractions. Some attribute "energy" to material objects that project a drain on our energy and focus, especially when these objects are no longer a relevant part of our lives. Items can also have a psychological pull on our attention that can distract us from our ability to focus and that slow us down at work. For example, if our office is filled with pictures of our children, past vacations, or other objects that represent significant parts of our lives, then when we sit down to work, our attention is pulled into memories and associations with those pictures and objects. This can make us less focused and productive when we need to get down to work.

I hate to say this, but it applies to classrooms as well. All those bright colors and displays that many teachers install in their classrooms every year may actually be undermining their students' ability to learn. There is a growing body of research that suggests that primary colors and bright bulletin boards and displays can overstimulate students. Like the pictures of our family vacations, these colors and displays draw students' attention away from learning. Instead, it is recommended that we use natural wood colors and softer primary colors that are more soothing and productive for kids (School Planning and Management, 2013).

Not convinced? Just think how good it feels to clear out your home, office, or classroom of unwanted and unneeded objects. Spring cleaning is an annual practice for a reason! The wave of relief we feel when we're not stumbling over stuff is pretty great, right? Just give it a try. In classrooms, see what impact it has on students for the classroom to be more streamlined and clear of clutter.

Emotional Freedom Techniques (EFT)

Emotional Freedom Techniques (EFT), also known as "tapping," is the combination of tapping acupressure points on the body while simultaneously stating phrases reflective of one's current emotional state. The statements we say while tapping are intended to acknowledge the negative or painful state we are in, and then to transform the limiting beliefs and statements we are telling ourselves into ones that are more positive and affirming. The tapping portion of EFT involves a sequence (or circuit) of tapping on the major meridian endpoints in the body, as identified in Chinese acupuncture (see Figure #4 below for the locations). These points include the blade of the hand, the top of the head, several places around the eye, under the nose, on the chin, on the collarbone, and on the side of the rib cage. When tapping and phrasing are paired together, they have been proven to calm the nervous system, bringing balance and energy to the body and rewiring the brain to respond in more healthy ways (Ortner, 2013). Some practitioners also claim that tapping has cured them of debilitating health and emotional issues that hadn't been able to be addressed through traditional Western medical and psychiatric methodologies prior.

Figure 4: EFT Tapping Points

Blade of hand

1: Eyebrow
2: Side of eye
3: Under Eye
4: Below nose
5: Chin
6: Chest, by collar bone
7: Side of chest below armpit
8: Top of head

Recent scientific research has sought to measure the effectiveness of tapping. This version of tapping is called *Clinical EFT*, and it has been validated in research studies to be a safe, fast, reliable, and effective treatment for both psychological and physical conditions (Church, 2013, pp. 651-52). Clinical EFT has also been proven effective for use with patients suffering from Post-Traumatic Stress Disorder and therefore could be used for people who are living with various traumas, including many of our students who live in neighborhoods marked by violence (Church, 2017). Used regularly, tapping has the potential to permanently reprogram our brains to eliminate the limiting beliefs and stress responses that cause us regular suffering and anxiety.

This application of tapping also fits perfectly with our 3 Eyes framework. Through intellect and insight, we are able to unearth the limiting beliefs, fears, and patterns that are getting in our way. Through tapping, we can rewire our responses to ones more aligned with our desires. Because tapping addresses the mental and emotional reactions we are having in the present moment, there is an infinite number of applications for it as an ongoing practice. The best way to learn more about tapping is to check it out on YouTube. If you search for Tapping or EFT, you will find 100's of free instructional videos and resources for how to apply it to your life and how to use it with children. I find that Brad Yates has a wide range of videos that are short, sweet, and effective (search *Tapping with Brad*).

Gratitude

Simply put, practicing gratitude means that we acknowledge and are thankful for the many gifts that are already present in our lives. There are many ways to practice gratitude; these include keeping a gratitude journal, saying thank you to another person in appreciation for something they have done for us, and sitting and reflecting on how elements of our lives have improved as compared to a time in the past. Law of Attraction expert Rhonda Byrne suggests we start and end our day with gratitude practices, and that whenever and however we can throughout the day, we give thanks for all of the gifts we are receiving (2012).

I recommend that before you start your day, ideally even before you finish your first cup of coffee, you jot down up to ten things that you are grateful for. This can be little things (like that cup of coffee), or bigger things like your job or family. It's okay to repeat the same ones each day, but if you can stretch yourself to find new things, you'll start seeing all of the many gifts that already surround you. Additionally, as many times as you can in between waking and sleeping, give thanks for all that you receive. This can be direct, such as thanking the shop person who rang up your purchase. This can also be in your mind, such silently giving thanks to the many people who maintain the sidewalk upon which you are walking.

For over a decade, gratitude expert Robert Emmons has studied the impact of gratitude on people between the ages of eight and 80. He's been able to show that a consistent gratitude practice leads to improved physical health (including stronger immune systems, lower blood pressure, and better sleep), psychological well-being (including higher levels of positive emotions and more joy, pleasure and optimism), and social connection (including being more helpful, generous and forgiving, and feeling less isolated and lonely) (2010).

Gratitude has two parts; it is an affirmation of goodness, and an acknowledgment of where that goodness comes from (Emmons, 2010). When we affirm goodness, we are paying attention to things in life that are positive. This isn't to say that we should ignore our challenges, but it is a reminder to create space to appreciate the gifts we are receiving in the middle of our challenges. When we acknowledge where the goodness comes from, it helps us to see that some of the positive things we're experiencing come from others. This acknowledgment helps us to see our connections with other people and to feel less alone (Emmons, 2010).

Beyond the benefits listed above, why is practicing gratitude a good thing? According to Emmons, here are a few additional benefits:

1. Gratitude allows us to celebrate the present moment and it magnifies positive emotions;
2. Gratitude blocks toxic and negative emotions;
3. Grateful people are more stress resistant; and
4. Grateful people have a higher sense of self-worth (2010).

Finally, research is demonstrating that gratitude is great for kids! When students practice gratitude, they have higher Grade Point Averages (GPAs), participate more in extra-curricular activities and have a stronger desire to contribute to society (Armenta, 2017). Students who express gratitude directly to parents and teachers feel more connected to them—a good thing when adolescents usually pull away from trusted adults (Arementa, 2017).

Gratitude has also been linked with decreased participation in high-risk behaviors in adolescents, including substance abuse and sexual behaviors.

I've had a daily gratitude practice for a couple of years now, and it has made a profound impact on my general well-being. I read somewhere that Einstein tried to say thank you at least 100 times a day, and I've taken on that same challenge. I say thank you a lot; often just in my head, but out loud when appropriate. I also keep a gratitude journal. When I think of it, I acknowledge the people I interact with and how they are supporting me. I also try to imagine and say thank you to all of the people, plants, and animals that contributed to something I am enjoying, such as my cup of coffee. Just think about it, to create my cup of coffee, nature helped out (with dirt, water, plants, and bees). So did lots and lots of people (the growers; the people who picked, dried, and roasted the beans; the people who ground and packaged the finished coffee; the delivery people who brought the coffee to the distributors and eventually to my house; and the people who help to keep my home going with electricity and clean running water). When I step back and consider the many contributions to my simple cup of coffee, it is difficult for me to feel isolated and alone.

Grounding or Earthing

This means spending time in nature and touching the earth. As humans, we have electrical energy currents running through our bodies, and our health and well-being are improved when we touch back in with the earth. It's like a giant battery, recharging us. Why is this important? Because of industrialized life, we have become separated from our daily connection with the earth. Now that most of us live in buildings and sleep in beds, we are far from the earth (sometimes very far in high-rises). We also wear rubber-soled shoes that block the grounding transmission that comes from the earth. This disconnect causes us to lose our grounding. To remedy this, we need to find ways to touch back in with the earth, ideally for about 30 minutes a day. Benefits of grounding include feeling more centered, balanced, and strong (Ober, 2018).

Not only does connecting with the earth provide significant benefits but so does being amongst the trees! In Japan, they have been doing a practice called *Forest Bathing* (just being in the presence of trees) for decades. In 1982, forest bathing became a part of Japan's national public health program (Livni, 2016). Japanese researchers who have studied the impact of forest bathing found that there are a lot of benefits, including promoting lower concentrations of cortisol (the stress hormone), lower pulse rate, and lower blood pressure (Livni, 2016). In other words, being in the forest is calming!

So, how can we Earth or Ground? Lots of ways! Take a walk in nature (ideally with your shoes off), walk amongst the trees, sit on the beach and watch the ocean, stop and smell the roses, garden. Hug a tree! I am fortunate enough to live along the water, which means that I get to walk by the ocean every day. I always feel calmer and more centered after breathing in the ocean air for a few minutes. I've also made it a goal to stop and smell the roses I pass as I walk my dogs and try to keep at least a few live plants in my home.

Intentions

An intention is a powerful way to set our desires into motion. This could be is a purpose, objective, or goal. According to doctor and spiritual teacher Deepak Chopra, intentions are the starting points of every dream, and everything that happens in the Universe begins with an intention (Chopra, 2018). When setting intentions, Chopra suggests a process that starts with a calming practice (such as meditation), stating your desired outcome (your intention), and then doing your best in the following hours, days and months to stay in the space of allowing for that intention to come true. Chopra suggests that we partner with the Universe to allow the intention to come to fruition, trusting that it will arrive at the right time and in the perfect way (2018).

In their book, Presence (2004), organizational management experts Peter Senge, et al., encourage what they call "crystallizing intent." When we crystallize intent, we are instantly open to the broader vision of our goal, while translating it into more concrete and refined intentions that can guide our actions (p. 133). With this process, successful change is led by people who are completely committed to the change. You gain momentum for the change by partnering with others that are similarly committed. The group's collective enthusiasm acts as the fuel to drive the change. This means that a for an intention to be realized, it must be clear, fully committed to, and supported by a group of people who also believe it is possible (those Believing Eyes that we discussed in the last chapter).

While Chopra talks about partnering with the Universe and Senge et al. discuss the power of a small group of committed people, in both examples setting an intention requires a clear vision for what we want and an unwavering belief that it will happen. When doubt or worry step in, we are unable to see what is possible and our options and prospects for success become limited.

Intention is the vision for something more. You can almost feel and taste that new thing. It is also trusting that it will come to be. Perhaps you set an intention to lose 20 pounds. While you go about losing the weight by eating healthier foods and exercising more, you also spend time each day envisioning how you will look and feel when the weight is gone. You create that vision of yourself as vividly as possible and try to live into that feeling without fixating on exactly when and how it will happen. You also absolutely avoid negative self-talk or attention on what you dislike about how you look now. Your goal is to stay in the aspirational state of what can be. Sprinkle in a little gratitude as if that state has already been achieved, and you're well on your way.

Journaling

Journaling is the practice of writing down one's thoughts and feelings. It's another fantastic way to capture the subconscious beliefs that are impacting our outlook. Journaling on a regular basis provides us with an outlet for expressing and exploring emotions, as well as a space to air thoughts and feelings that we may be scared to share with others. There is also a wealth of research proving that expressing emotional or traumatic events through journaling leads to improvements in health, psychological well-being, and physiological functioning (Ullrich and Lutgendorf, 2002).

Those who have studied the impact of journaling say that it is beneficial, in part, because ignoring or suppressing a negative event is stressful to the body and prevents one from being able to develop a healthy outlook. Through journaling we gain a sense of control and perspective over the challenging situations we encounter, allowing us to regain some sense of equilibrium (Ullrich and Lutgendorf, 2002). I am often surprised at what comes out when I let myself just write. Not only do I feel better, but also, I usually gain insights into what is bothering me or find solutions to challenges I am facing. The act of writing pulls that information out of my subconscious mind and brings it to my conscious attention.

Meditation

Meditation is the practice of calming one's mind, bringing attention back to the body, and monitoring one's breath. Meditation is a centuries-old practice perhaps made most famous by the Buddha. He cultivated a meditation practice to help him to stay present and centered when confronted with the challenges that are a part of living life, including having desires and facing illness and death. It's also probably the most well-known of the mindfulness practices.

There are many different versions of meditation, from ones that encourage us to practice breathing in, holding our breath, and breathing out in a timed sequence, to ones that are more involved and include visualizations that accompany the breaths. Whatever style you practice, the goal is to bring yourself into the present moment and to allow your thoughts to pass by without letting them hook you.

Neuroscientist and founder of the Center for Healthy Minds, Dr. Richard Davidson, says that there are four elements to well-being that are enhanced through a regular meditation practice: resilience, outlook, attention, and generosity. A large body of scientific research shows that deliberate practice in these four areas contributes to a general improved state of well-being. Through our effortful attention and a regular meditation practice, we can produce a more general state of well-being all the time (Davidson, 2016).

Today, meditation is a socially-acceptable practice in the United States. The cool part is that it's also been gaining ground in our classrooms and schools. Use of meditation with students has proven to lower discipline issues in schools and has supported students living with trauma to have tools to regulate their emotions. Additionally, according to Mindful Schools, a nonprofit organization that provides mindfulness training to students and teachers, "when teachers learn mindfulness, they not only reap personal benefits such as reduced stress and burnout, [but they also] reported greater efficacy in doing their jobs and had more emotionally supportive classrooms and better classroom organization" (Mindful Schools, 2017).

According to Deepak Chopra (2018), "most of the time our mind is caught up in thoughts, emotions, and memories. Beyond this noisy internal dialogue is a state of pure awareness that is sometimes referred to as 'the gap.' One of the most effective tools we have for entering the gap is meditation. Meditation takes you beyond the ego-mind into the silence and stillness of pure consciousness." In other words, through meditation, we are able to step back from the constant churning in our minds and gain enough space to tap into the information and experiences in the present moment. When we can do that, we are less tied to our habitual responses and interpretations. Instead, we can be open to information that we haven't yet explored. And, we can take advantage of the space between stimulus and response. Finally, there is also evidence that meditating on a regular basis reduces the amygdala (our fight or flight center) and enlarges our hippocampus and prefrontal cortex centers of the brain. These changes increase our ability to regulate our emotions and retain a more balanced and calmer frame of mind over the long term (Mindful Schools, 2017).

Mirror Work

This is the practice of looking deep into one's eyes and repeating affirmations. Affirmations are statements of fact, stated in the present tense. For example, "I am beautiful." Positive affirmations are healing and support positive self-esteem, while negative affirmations reinforce our fears, doubts, and self-criticisms. Yes, for those of you who are Saturday Night Live fans and are old enough to remember Al Franken's portrayal of Stuart Smalley, this is what he did. If you're not familiar, look it up, it's pretty funny! My favorite is when Stuart Smalley interviews Michael Jordan. In the sketches, Stuart Smalley faces himself in the mirror and says things like, "I am good enough, I'm smart enough, and darn it, I like myself!" Stuart Smalley is portrayed as being highly sensitive and a bit needy, and he makes mirror work look pretty silly. It's not! Consider the possibilities...

According to author and spiritual teacher, Louise Hay, we are all already doing mirror work, just usually as a way to beat ourselves up. Those repetitive, and mostly negative, thoughts that we have running most of the time *are* affirmations. Think of the number of times you've looked at yourself in the mirror and criticized some part of yourself for being imperfect, or criticized yourself in your mind for making a mistake.

We have explored self-talk already in our discussion of Insight and learned a note-taking practice for catching the habitual thoughts that are running in our minds, almost as if on autopilot (our Pokemon example). Through mirror work, we gain another strategy for catching those thoughts as well as a process for changing them. We first identify the habitual negative patterns of thought we are having and then replace the disempowering thoughts for ones that allow us to have more self-love and confidence.

According to Hay, the most powerful affirmations are the ones we say out loud when we are in front of a mirror (2016, p. 1). Mirrors reflect our feelings back to ourselves and provide us with immediate feedback and insight as to what we are telling ourselves. Hay asserts that the more we practice mirror work, then the more we learn to take care of ourselves on a deeper level. Rather than standing in front of the mirror, criticizing ourselves for our love handles and crow's feet, for example, we learn to go to the mirror to tell ourselves positive things, such as thanking ourselves for something we've accomplished. With enough repetition and practice (Hay recommends 21 consecutive days when you start this practice) you will learn how to become your own cheerleader and build self-compassion and confidence.

If you're not ready to jump into a 21-day affirmation practice, consider just saying "I love you" to yourself whenever you look into the mirror. Also, try to catch the messages you are currently telling yourself when you look at your reflection. This simple shift should help you to feel more grounded and connected with yourself. Also, want a cooler frame of reference for mirror work than Stuart Smalley? Check out singer and songwriter Theresa Perez who sings a song called, "Sweetest I Love You," which talks about giving oneself more compassion through saying I Love You in the mirror. In one line of the song she says, "I look in the mirror, say I love you, deep into my eyes, so I know it's true. 'Cuz my soul is yearning to hear it from me. Can't nobody make a difference if I don't feel it too" (Perez, 2007). Theresa's right. Gaining the love we seek from others begins with loving ourselves! Also, I much prefer believing that my mirror work looks more like Theresa's than Stuart's!

Movement

Get moving! Walking, running, stretching, practicing yoga, swimming... all of these and more will provide us with a chance to connect back in with our bodies and to treat them with care. If you haven't exercised in a while, start small and build up. If you work in a particularly stressful environment, rather than eating your lunch at your desk, get out and take a walk. Are your students being too wiggly or sluggish? Take a stretch break. When my middle school students were particularly difficult to focus, sometimes we got out and took a five-minute walk around the yard or just stood up and shook out our limbs. We might have lost a few minutes of instruction time, but we more than gained it back in the level of connection and concentration when we started back again.

I want to give you a specific example regarding yoga. Various research studies have shown that regular exposure to the movements and breathing practices found in yoga is good for kids from primary school through college. Through regular practice, students showed decreased stress levels and improved academic achievement, memory, and attention span (Booe, 2018). Like meditation, yoga is also making its way into our schools, and it's a good thing. Just the other day, I was walking through one of the schools in my district, and they had posters in the hallways and on classroom doors with stick figures doing yoga stretches. The encouragement on the poster was to use stretching as a way to feel better emotionally and physically. At the school where I was an assistant principal, our second graders did yoga as a part of their weekly exercise regime. Outside of the yoga practice, I'd see those same kids stretching and breathing when they were upset—the posters come to life!

Prayer

Like intentions or affirmations, prayer provides us with an opportunity to both say what we want or need and to release control of the outcome. Based on one's religious beliefs, prayers can take many forms and are used for a variety of purposes. Many people claim to have experienced (or helped to produce) spontaneous medical healings as a result of prayer, and prayer gives many of us great comfort. Since this is such a personal practice and one that is tied to unique traditions and ceremonies, I won't say more here. I will caution that unless you work in a non-public school where prayer is a named part of the curriculum that parents have agreed to, it should not be used with or in front of students.

Visualization

When we visualize an event, we try to create it in as much detail as possible. We try to conjure the sights, smells, textures, sounds, physical sensations, and emotions as realistically as possible. You can see this clearly with athletes. Michael Phelps before a swim, who sits with his eyes closed and music on, playing out every stroke of his swim. Stephen Curry stands at the free throw line, bouncing the basketball a few times, setting his body and picturing the shot going in. The key to visualization is to create as clear a picture and emotional connection as you can to your desired outcome. What will it look like? How will you feel when you have it? Every time doubt or fear comes up, acknowledge the feelings that doubt brings up. Then, try to move back into the desired space with as much clarity as possible.

Wrapping it Up

For the most part, mindfulness practices like those described above are free, easy to do, and can be used to benefit both our students and ourselves. The goal with establishing any mindfulness practice is to be more fully in our bodies and in the present moment. Our minds are incredibly powerful, and when we spend too much time either reliving the past or anticipating the future, we miss the treasure and opportunities the present moment provides. Mindfulness gives us a way to return to the present.

Before using any of the above with students, I encourage you to look more deeply into how to put them into practice. Where available, partner with experts who can help you to use these techniques safely and effectively with students. I also recommend that you seek parent, guardian, and leadership permission before introducing them. Several organizations provide programming and research related to bringing mindful practices to children. Two places to check out are Roots of Empathy and Mindful Schools. There are also established nationwide programs that focus on students' emotional well-being, including Restorative Justice, Social-Emotional Learning, and Positive Behavioral Interventions & Supports. Each of these programs come with a host of training materials, best practices, and tools for introducing them in the classroom.

Make it Yours:

What mindfulness-boosting strategy calls to you? Pick one that you'll try out for the next couple of weeks and see how it makes you feel. Try to do it at the same time each day so that it can be easy to remember. Have fun!

The Power of the 3 Eyes

Now that we know a bit more about how to access our intuition through mindfulness let's put it to work! The contents in this section will provide some ways to put on our 3-D glasses by intentionally bringing the gifts of Intellect, Insight, and Intuition together. Like He-man as he raises his sword skyward and proclaims, "By the Power of Grayskull, I HAVE THE POWER!," so do we! To put that power to good use, we will revisit our Theories of Action for using the 3 Eyes to bring about great personal and school-wide transformations. Here they are:

- **Self-Work:** If we use the 3 Eyes (Intellect, Insight, and Intuition) to see our lives and learned responses with more clarity and embark on a process to lovingly "rewire" the areas that do not align with who we want to be, then we experience greater self-appreciation and motivation to change. When we do that, we can realize our individual goals and engage with others to transform our educational settings.
- **School-Work:** If use the 3 Eyes to identify areas for needed improvement in our schools, and we create communities founded on trust and accountability, then we can use the power of teams to address the areas of needed change. When we do that, we can transform our educational settings into ones that support the adults and students alike to realize their potential.

Through the use of the 3 Eyes, we gain free will and can quite literally change how our brains are wired. Through Intellect, we learn how to differentiate between our conscious and subconscious thoughts and how to step out of our learned responses to act as an observer. When we can observe ourselves (almost like an objective third party), then Insight aids us to understand what beliefs are operating in our subconscious minds and how they show up in our daily lives. Insight also helps us to catch repeated patterns that get in our way and to identify past strategies that have enabled us to realize our goals. With Intuition, we first learn to quiet our minds so that we can access information that our busy minds can miss. As we will see below, Intuition is also the playground for manifestation. Like David Lynch describes, Intuition is the place where emotion and intellect come together, and with the aid of imagination, we can envision and live into a new way of being. Table four below shows how our theories of action have shown up so far in this book.

Table 4: Theory of Action—in Action

	Intellect	Insight	Intuition	Outcome
Function	Cognitive abilities; aids in identifying limiting patterns, thoughts, or areas of improvement; executive control.	A deep understanding of our habitual programming, beliefs, and emotions.	Quieting the mind and reconnecting with the body to access new and different information. Use of imagination to envision a new reality.	Mobilization of all three lenses to envision and align ourselves to a new reality; the Law of Attraction.
Source of Information	Conscious Mind	Subconscious Mind	Body and Soul	Full mind-body-soul integration that leads to manifestation.
Physical Location	Head-Brain	Heart-Brain	Gut-Brain	Aligned beliefs and realization of our desires.

As we have moved through the book, we've unpacked each of the 3 Eyes in detail and developed a baseline understanding of how each lens shows up and influences us. Now it is time to show how the three lenses can work together. To do this, we will apply the concepts we have already discussed to the Law of Attraction and manifestation. Word of warning: for some of us, this may feel like a journey into the improbable. Some of us may label what is discussed below as uber woo-woo or as magical thinking. That's just our intellects (with heavy influence from our egos) talking. In reality, what we'll be talking about is harnessing three innate skills we already have within in us. Rather than magical thinking, the real fairy dust being used is intentionality. Using the 3 Eyes on purpose rather than by default or by accident.

The Law of Attraction

The Law of Attraction states that what you focus upon you bring to yourself. According to Rhonda Byrne, an expert on the **Law of Attraction**, "in your life, the law operates on your thoughts and feelings, because they are energy too, and so whatever you think, whatever you feel, you attract to you" (2012, pg. 7). **Manifestation** is the process by which something theoretical is made real. Manifestation occurs when something we feel, think or desire becomes realized in some tangible way. For example, imagine that you want a new car. Through hard work, saving your money, and remaining focused on your goal, eventually that new car becomes a reality; you've manifested a new car.

Throughout the book, we have discussed how our thoughts and feelings create our realities—this is the Law of Attraction at work. If I have a subconscious belief (given to me as a child) that I have an uncontrollable temper, for example, then the way that I interpret circumstances and see myself reinforce that belief. As I move through the world, I keep finding myself in situations where my temper takes over, where I lose control. I have a coworker that pushes every last button. I marry a partner who enrages me. The more experiences I manifest that reinforce this subconscious program, the more that belief takes hold, and on and on I go.

The Law of Attraction works in the positive direction as well. If I have a belief that I can accomplish anything that I dream of, then I likewise send that signal out into the world. My subconscious mind helps to create experiences to reinforce this belief. As a result, I find that I reach my goals with ease and push myself farther and farther, feeling unstoppable.

To put the Law of Attraction to work for us, we need to learn to think in a different way. This is where imagination comes in. To change the programming and the messages we tell ourselves, we need to be able to imagine (with as much clarity and emotional attachment as possible) an alternate reality to the one we live day in and day out. To do this, we focus on the change we seek from the inside-out through our thoughts, rather than waiting for our external world to change to make our dreams come true. In other words, if we want to feel happy, instead of waiting for something outside of ourselves to make us happy (such as an ice cream cone, a drink or our soulmate), we conjure that happy feeling within ourselves. The outside world then brings experiences to our lives that reflect our inner state of happiness.

We've all done this. Have you ever noticed how much more smoothly your day or your classroom go when you are in a good mood? The parking space is there just before you are late for your appointment. Your students behave wonderfully during the principal's observation of your class. People on the street smile at you as you pass. Birds flit down and lift the hem of your cape before it trails in the mud. The opposite is also true. When we're in a bad mood, almost as if by magic, we find ourselves behind the slowest person on the freeway who changes lanes whenever we do. Our students cannot seem to accomplish even the most mundane tasks without arguments and issues breaking out. The car drives by splashes the puddled rainwater in the drain on our new outfit.

How do we get the Law of Attraction to work for us? According to Bryne:

> "The law of attraction says that we can't make a problem go away by focusing on it, because focusing on the problem can only make the problem worse. Instead, we should do the exact opposite, and focus on the ideal state [of what we want to change]... and give our thoughts and feelings to that" (2012, pg. 153).

Dr. Joe Dispenza has extensively studied how to use our minds to create our realities. He adds to Bryne's advice by saying that focusing on our desire is not enough. We also must not focus on *how* our desire will be realized (2012). To manifest our desires, we need to be able to envision a reality that we currently are not experiencing while also letting go of how we will get it. Why let go? Simply put, if we knew how to get what we wanted, we'd have it already! When we try to figure out how we'll get our desires, we retrieve all those old programs that haven't worked thus far to bring us what we want. When we let go of the how, we allow for new possibilities, new ways of having our desire come to life. If we already knew how to lose those extra 20 pounds, find the love of our lives, or create a welcoming and productive learning environment for our students, then we wouldn't have that desire in the first place, right?

Dispenza says that when we can move into a state of expectant allowing, then we move from, "cause and effect (waiting for something outside of you to make a change inside of you) to causing an effect (changing something inside of you to produce an effect outside of you)" (2012, p. 26). This is a more empowered and proactive stance towards life. Finally, Bryne and Dispenza both encourage us to add a healthy dose of gratitude to the process. Gratitude is the real magic dust all of us have been looking for. When we are grateful as if the thing we desire has already occurred, we send a message to our brains that this is our new reality. When we do that, we retrain our brains to accept this reality as the new normal. Our subconscious minds start looking for evidence to reinforce this new reality, thus making it stronger and stronger.

Big Idea #17:

What we focus our thoughts and feeling upon we bring to ourselves.

Make it Yours:

Think back to one of those days that either went really well or really poorly.

List out a few of the events that happened that day. Can you trace back to how your day started? Can you make a connection between your thoughts and your lived reality?

Here's an example from my life. Recently, I was in search of a new home for my family. I had sold my house to prepare for this, with the plan of downsizing to a place closer to the water and my son's school. Within a month of me selling my house, the market in the San Francisco Bay Area went up by 20%! This meant that not only did I not get the full value for my home, but the places that I could easily purchase just a month before were suddenly out of reach. Having fully expected that we'd find a place soon, my son, dogs, and I were staying in a small apartment with most of our belongings in storage. I was faced with the prospect of having to live there for years until I could save more money or until the market settled down. This put me into a full-on panic on multiple levels.

As a student of the Law of Attraction, however, I decided to try it out. What could it hurt, right? So, I sat down, and I wrote out exactly what I was looking for, including size, location, and outdoor space for my dogs. I then tried to imagine how I would feel when I found that place (excited, yet calm and confident). Every time I started to panic and worry over how I was going to find a place, I did my best to return to that feeling of already having found my new home. I also expressed gratitude for already having it.

I'll admit there were times when I focused on the wrong things. I spent days in deep worry and despair, waking up in the middle of the night feeling anxious and unable to imagine that I could possibly find a place in such a market. Nonetheless, like when meditating, I did my best to acknowledge the negative thoughts and feelings but then let them go before they could take hold. As much as I could, I returned to the feeling of living in my new home now. I also applied a strategy I learned from spiritual teacher Abraham-Hicks, envisioning my new place like a seed, imagining it eventually rising out the ground like a cornstalk when the timing was right.

I know it might sound kind of silly, but it really helped me to appreciate that timing is essential, and that like a seed, you don't see the plant manifest right away. The seed needs to split open and grow roots. The actual ear on a stalk is the last evidence of the corn. Just like we don't plant fully-grown corn stalks into the ground, the same is true for our desires. For my place to manifest, I needed to trust that I had planted the seed (imagining my desired home, feeling what it would feel like to have it, and expressing gratitude that I received it). It was now in the soil of the field of possibilities, taking root and preparing to be visible.

And guess what? It worked! Just as I had resigned myself to living in our tiny apartment for a few years and accepted that my home would come when the timing was right, it showed up! Not only did I find the perfect place that met all of my requirements, but I had an accepted offer *under* asking and far below similar homes in the area. No joke.

If we learn how to direct our conscious thoughts and emotions on our desires, then we can create the reality of our dreams. The potential for how to apply the Law of Attraction to our own lives and to any challenge is infinite. We just need to focus on what is possible.

There's a Neural Pathway for That...

The Law of Attraction not your thing? No worries, we can just go in and change your brain! Throughout the book, we've discussed the idea of rewiring our brains to dispel limiting beliefs and to think in new and more empowering ways. While this idea of "rewiring" works nicely with our metaphor of brains as computers, there is a literal connection as well. Our brains can grow and change. This applies to both the discrete functions of parts of our brains, as well as how information is communicated within the brain. Not only does this happen naturally, but we can also consciously choose to "rewire" our computers. Called **self-directed neuroplasticity**, and this is when we use our minds to change the way our brain works so that we can change the mind for the better (Hanson, 2011). Wait, what?? Let's take this in pieces, starting with how information is communicated in our brains.

As we have discussed, our minds are always on alert, measuring our level of safety and connectedness. **Mind** refers to the information that gets transmitted within our bodies, including our thoughts and sensory information (sights, smells, tastes, physical sensations, and sounds). While most of the 40 million bits of information we take in per second is registered on a subconscious level, and only a fraction reaches our conscious awareness (about 40 bits), repeated processing of the same kinds of information shapes the structure of the brain—creating the "wiring" in our computers. This happens because the areas of the brain that are the most triggered by the information we are processing get more blood, and neurons that repeatedly fire together (communicate information between each other) develop stronger bonds (Hanson, 2011).

Neurons are cells that communicate information about our environment and the physical or emotional state we are in. Neurons send this information from one neuron to another neuron or to a part of the body. As neurons communicate consistently with one another, they form **neural pathways**, which can be thought of as paths upon which information travels. Like a path on a hiking trail, the more a neural pathway is used, the deeper and more defined it becomes. This means that our repeated thoughts and sensory responses form strong neural pathways. These pathways communicate information to the brain, which in turn shapes the structures and areas of the brain. The cool thing is that if we want to change those neural pathways, we can!

Neuroplasticity is the ability for the brain to grow and change in response to the way we use it. Depending on the size and activity of parts of our brains, or the repetitive thoughts and emotions we have, neuroplasticity can, therefore, have positive or negative consequences to our physical, mental and emotional well-being. While all of this is happening within our heads, it can be helpful to see neuroplasticity as creating changes in the brain from the inside-out (structures in our brain influencing our thoughts and feelings) and/or from the outside-in (focusing our thoughts and feelings to produce changes in the structures of our brains).

Here are two examples of how the size and shape of parts of the brain affect our lived experience, influencing us from the inside-out. In this first example, imagine that our left prefrontal cortex is enlarged. I know this is a tricky visual. The prefrontal cortex is located at the upper front of the brain, and the left side is responsible for inhibiting the experience of negative emotions. While it may be difficult to imagine what that part of the brain looks like, try to imagine it as a pumped-up bodybuilder. Just as a bodybuilder who repeatedly performs bicep curls will produce stronger biceps, the stronger the left prefrontal cortex of the brain gets, the more it can perform its function to suppress negative emotions. Our active (pumped up) left prefrontal cortex causes us to experience fewer negative emotions and to experience more happy emotions as a result (Hanson, 2011).

Now imagine that we are chronically under high degrees of stress. When we experience stress, our bodies release cortisol (known as the stress hormone), and repeated experiences of stress means that cortisol is pumping through our bodies on a regular basis. If we were to look inside our brains, we would see that the constant presence of cortisol has acted almost like battery acid, eating away at our hippocampus and causing its overall size to decrease (Hanson, 2011). When our hippocampus is reduced in size, it is inhibited from doing its job, which is to evaluate and respond to threats and to store both short-term and long-term memories. This means that if we are chronically stressed, we are more likely to remain so, and our ability to store and retrieve memories is diminished. If we return to the bodybuilder analogy, our muscles have atrophied, and as a result, we are inhibited from performing at even average standards.

In both cases, the pumped-up prefrontal cortex and the atrophied hippocampus, the size and level of activity of discrete parts of our brains affect our emotions and cognitive interpretation of our experiences. The over- or under-development of these parts of our brains leads to ongoing experiences of the same state. While it is normal for humans to experience stress in response to external factors, because our internal processes are compromised (staying at high alert and pumping out extra amounts of cortisol) we experience heightened degrees of stress. The same is true with the well-developed prefrontal cortex; we can pump-up this area of our brains by focusing on positive things, but we have a head start because that area is already working at high capacity.

The mind can also influence the structure of the brain, producing a change from the outside-in. A famous example of how mental activity can shape our brains is taxi drivers in London. To become a certified taxi driver in London, all drivers must memorize the complex network of streets that make up the city. Before and after brain scans of these taxi drivers have shown that as a result of all of that intentional memorization, their hippocampus (the area of the brain responsible for memory) are measurably thicker than before their training began (Hanson, 2011). In other words, the intentional focus on memorizing the streets of London increased the part of the brain that is responsible for storing memories; they pumped up their hippocampus!

While neuroplasticity can occur passively, without conscious effort or attention, with self-directed neuroplasticity, we can intentionally create a change in the wiring and functioning of parts of our brains. This happens because, for better or worse, neurons become stronger when they are under our attention (Hanson, 2011). For example, if our thoughts are constantly on the negative and challenging parts of our lives, we strengthen those neural pathways and the parts of our brains that respond to threats and stress, making those parts stronger and stronger (the diminished hippocampus example from above). If, on the other hand, we intentionally focus on gratitude and positive things, this attention similarly acts like steroids when building muscles, enhancing our ability to develop those parts of our brains, such as with the enlarged left prefrontal cortex example we discussed.

Do you recall our discussion about the Law of Attraction? What you focus upon you bring to yourself? This is the physical explanation for how the Law works. While this kind of thinking may not bring about a new home, consciously directing our attention on the thoughts and feelings we want to experience does change the way our brains function. With deliberate effort, over time we can change the habitual thoughts and reactions that we no longer want to experience.

How do we turn on self-directed neuroplasticity? Mindfulness and meditation! Brain scans of people who have a regular meditation practice show that they have three pumped up areas of their brains. The first area is called the insula, and it is located on the left and the right sides towards the front of our brains. The insula is involved with our ability to do something called interoception, which means the ability to tune into the inner state of our bodies (such as whether we are hungry, thirsty, hot or cold) as well as tune into our deep feelings (Hanson, 2013). The second area is in the prefrontal cortex, and it is the part of the brain that controls our ability to focus our attention, and the third is the somatosensory cortex, which also helps us to tune into our bodies (Hanson, 2013).

Similar to working out at the gym to build muscle, people with regular meditation practices have well-developed parts of their brains that aid them in having a stronger mind-body connection, greater emotional awareness and an improved ability to focus their attention. If this wasn't good enough, meditation also stalls the aging process of the brain. Brain scans of long-term meditators have shown that over time, their brain mass remains the same size while non-meditators' brain mass decreased as they aged (Hanson, 2013).

While the positive implications of a regular meditation practice are many, if we return to this notion of self-directed neuroplasticity, the possibilities are profound. As discussed, through meditating we work out three areas of our brains (our insula, an area in the prefrontal cortex, and our somatosensory cortex), thereby improving our self-awareness and focus. With improved awareness and focus, not only are we more aware of the thoughts and feelings that are running in the background and influencing our experiences, but also we can focus our attention on the thoughts and feelings we want to have instead. When we can be more intentional about our thoughts, we are empowered to rewire the neural pathways in our brains to decrease the habitual thoughts that are negative, harmful, or are just not aligned with our conscious desires. We can also pump up those pathways that we desire to have instead. This is the ultimate way that we can regain free will over the thoughts and reactions that have been installed in our subconscious minds. Through time and attention, we can shape the experiences we want to have!

Note: I know we got into a lot of brainy stuff just now. There's a Brain Primer in the appendix that may help you to understand a bit more about how all of this works.

Big Idea #18:

Through meditation, mindfulness, and intentionality, we can rewire the parts of our brains that have a negative influence on our thoughts and feelings.

Implications

Intuition is the final piece of the puzzle when it comes to understanding our lives with more perspective and for creating different outcomes. Through mindfulness, we learn to slow down our thoughts and connect back into the present moment. When we're in the present moment, we're able to access new sources of information and insights that we cannot retrieve when we are so caught up in reliving the past or anticipating the future. Intuition is also the fertile ground for creating a new reality. By combining our thoughts (intellect) with our emotions (insight) and by imagining a new reality (intuition), we can manifest our goals and dreams.

Self-Work:

Through mindfulness, we can build a more profound and more grounded relationship with ourselves and the people and world around us. When we feel more grounded and connected, we also feel happier and more able to realize our goals.

By learning how to connect with our intuition, we are afforded a whole new level of information to support us to make clearer, more empowered, and aligned choices in our lives.

When we use the power of the Law of Attraction and self-directed neuroplasticity, we can rewire our habitual thoughts and patterns to be in alignment with who and what we want to be. This gives us the power of choice over our subconscious programming.

School-Work:

Mindfulness practices are gaining ground in educational settings, (including gratitude, yoga, meditation, and tapping). Use of these practices help students to feel more grounded, clear, and focused; resulting in improved learning and achievement outcomes.

Mindfulness has been proven to reverse the impact of implicit bias. By supporting our teachers and leaders to participate in mindfulness practices, not only will they feel better overall, but they will be better able to detect and interrupt implicit biases that would otherwise cloud their judgment and treatment of their students.

Even in an ordinarily chaotic classroom, there are moments of calm. When teachers can put their attention on those moments, they can increase those incidents of calm through the power of the Law of Attraction.

Perspective matters. Shifting from a deficit-based to an assets-based point of view can have a transformative effect on our outlook and ability to create the changes we seek. Educators are trained to focus on what is wrong and to fix it (i.e., my kids can't read so I am going to teach them how to). While this kind of analysis has a place and serves a purpose in education, it also directs our attention to what we don't want or what our students are unable to achieve. What would it look like to focus on what is right and trying to expand upon that instead? In other words, my students know their ABCs, so what can I do to build on this skill so that they can read? How might this shift in language and perspective change the way that we communicate (both verbally and nonverbally) to our students? How might an assets-based frame impact our perception of our kids' ability to achieve? How might this shift manifest in improved outcomes for kids?

And so the Warrior's Path Begins...

At the end of the last chapter, I talked about how my worldview was cracked open as I began a spiritual journey. We explored the transition I made from living in my head to living more in my heart. With that, I also shifted my focus to love and gratitude and away from a sole reliance on logic and intellect. While my perspective was starting to change, I wasn't sure how to reconcile it with the life I had created.

Still being intellectually-oriented, I did what any good researcher does, I started learning as much as I could about my new-found spirituality! As I read works from various teachers, some common themes began emerging. The first was the healing power of love; it lies at the basis of real transformation. The second was the power of beliefs to influence how we experience our lives. The third was the influence that our thoughts and feelings have on the trajectory of our lives. Once I started making a shift on the inside to integrate these themes, my outer world also began to change.

Being the Believing Eyes

While I have always loved my colleagues, I will admit that for much of my career, I have also competed with and judged many of them. When I began my spiritual journey, I started to see how prevalent this judgment and competition was amongst the people I worked with, and how it undermined our ability to connect and be vulnerable with one another. I also started noticing just how bad I felt when I participated in that kind of activity; physically, emotionally, and psychologically. I'd walk away from those conversations feeling heavy and anxious and fearful. I'd have this feeling of looking back over my shoulder, wondering when I was going to be the one talked about next. As well, I began doubting the authenticity of the complements and kindnesses I experienced. With my new awareness about beliefs and the Law of Attraction, I resolved to start changing the conversations and how I treated my colleagues.

I began a practice of being the Believing Eyes for my friends and colleagues. When a colleague experienced success at work, I cheered for them. When I was excited to see someone I cared about, I told them so. While at first, this was more of an intentional "fake it until you make it" kind of thing, very quickly it came easily and the competition I felt towards my peers faded away. While I continued to have goals for my career trajectory, I no longer felt that those needed to come at the expense of others. Rather, I came to see that it would come in collaboration with others. More often than not, my shift to being the Believing Eyes for others was cause for them to appreciate their own accomplishments alongside me. It also came with the added benefit that Sonia Choquette said it would, it brought multitudes of Believing Eyes back to me! Since becoming the Believing Eyes, most days are filled with smiles and hugs, even when times are tough.

Beliefs in Action

A big part of my work over the years has been to observe and to provide feedback on classroom instruction. As someone who naturally "got" classroom management and how to break down lessons into teachable parts, I often struggled with how to guide the teachers I observed to change their practice, especially when it came to establishing positive and productive classroom cultures. I found that no matter how specifically I provided the feedback and how well that feedback was implemented, some teachers persisted in struggling to establish order and community in their classrooms. This had baffled me for years, and I will admit that I wrote off those experiences with the notion that some people were just natural teachers and some weren't.

I held this thought until I started learning about the power of beliefs. All of a sudden, the same failed lessons were no longer evidence of a teacher's innate abilities, but rather, examples of beliefs playing out right before me. First, I saw it in myself. I started to see that if I didn't believe that I could effectively support a teacher to change their practice, then I tended to be less generous with my time. While I'd still provide the contractual amount of hours of support and followed the procedures by the book, I noticed that I didn't go the extra mile if I didn't believe I could help them.

I also saw the power of beliefs in the teachers themselves. I could see how some of their limiting beliefs about themselves or their kids undermined their efforts. If they didn't believe that their classrooms could improve, even if they implemented my suggested actions to the letter, their lessons still failed in one way or another. In our post-observation discussions, themes of self-doubt or blaming the students emerged. I could see how their lack of belief in themselves and/or in their students kept them in a painful cycle. Rather than feeling anger or frustration like I would have in the past, I felt deep empathy for all involved. I felt for the teacher whose beliefs caused them to experience days filled with stress and disappointment. I felt for the kids whose potential was being cut short by adults who did not see all that they could be. I felt for all involved, including the whole school system that created and reinforced so many of these outcomes.

I also felt hope. I quickly saw that so much of what I was learning about the beliefs and the Law of Attraction could be applied to my work, and thus to the genesis of this book.

Seeing is Believing

Since integrating the 3 Eyes into my life, I have seen considerable improvements in my sense of calm and clarity. While writing this book, I have been in the midst of profound personal and professional transitions. This includes yet another possible layoff due to budget issues in my school district. Here is where the power of the Universe is at play. While I have been working on this book for over a year, it is significant that I'm wrapping it up while going through yet another potential job transition. If you'll recall, I began this journey following three successive job transitions, and concluding my book with a possible fourth has provided me with the gift of perspective.

Let's be real. I've still got lots of work to do. Working within the context of impending budget cuts has made for a challenging work environment (again!). I've certainly had moments of anxiety and worry about being able to take care of my son and have had feelings of anger at my district for putting so many people in this position. Under all of it, however, like a gentle stream, there has also been a sense of calm, of trust and of self-confidence that I did not have three years ago.

While the circumstances around losing my job are very similar to the first time my school district had to consolidate positions, this time I haven't made it about me. I am sure that part of this is just that I'm good at getting laid off by now! For better or worse I've gotten accustomed to this kind of change, and I know that the world won't come to an end. More profoundly, is in how I am integrating this new space of groundlessness. While in the three previous job transitions, I used the circumstances as fodder for beating myself up, this time I feel incredibly calm and grateful. Most of the time, I trust that all of this is happening for a reason. Instead of focusing on my hurt and pain, I have been focusing on the positive moments I am having with my colleagues and have been looking for the opportunities that exist within this challenge.

For me, this marks a significant shift. More than anything else, what I've noticed this time around is how much more I love myself! While in the past, I took the job transitions personally and allowed old beliefs and patterns to rule my mind, this time I am holding myself close, and do not see this as a personal failure at all. Instead, I have become the person that others are coming to for support and reassurance, and I am not distracted all the time with my pain. I am also using this transition as an invitation to step into even more challenges. While I watch my colleagues scramble for jobs or for a place in the dwindling organizational structure, I have decided to take a risk on myself and start my own business. For the first time in my life, I am okay with not knowing exactly what the future holds and I am curious and excited about what will come next.

Finally, I am spending far more time in the present moment, enjoying the richness of what already is, rather than on worrying about what will be. I really do stop and smell the roses, send a silent thank you to the Universe when I catch myself having a wonderful time, and I laugh a lot. As with any significant change, I still have times where the old patterns take-over. Worry, doubt, and self-criticism can still rule the day. But those days are fewer, and the grip of those thoughts and feelings are less extreme than they once were. Even better, the level of connection I feel to all living kind continues to deepen and my feelings of alienation are fading away. I am genuinely able to see and experience my life with more depth and clarity. This is the promise of the 3 Eyes, and why I felt compelled to write about them. If I can have such profound a transformation, and in such a short period of time, then I know that you can too.

Putting It All Together

"Change will not come if we wait for some other person, or if we wait for some other time. We are the ones we've been waiting for. We are the change that we seek." Barack Obama

Looking Back

In the previous chapter on Intuition, we learned how important mindfulness is in bringing us into the present moment. When we are present, we can access our intuitive gifts more easily, and therefore have a deeper source of information to draw upon. We also learned that intuition is the final piece in the puzzle for envisioning and realizing a new way of being. When we combine our cognitive abilities (Intellect), with a deep understanding of ourselves and our emotions (Insight) and use mindfulness to access untapped information (Intuition), we can conceive of new ideas and envision a future different than our current reality.

Looking Forward

Now we're going to put all of the pieces together. We will start by setting the groundwork for a successful transformation effort—bringing the subconscious and conscious minds together. Then, we will go about this change process through the use of a Cycle of Inquiry (COI). We'll start by explaining what a COI is and why it's beneficial to changing beliefs. Next, we'll look at each step in the cycle in detail. Throughout, we'll discuss how a COI can be applied to our self-work and school-work, and end with suggestions for how to start off on this journey. Let's go!

And so, drumroll please, it's time to introduce our final pair of glasses! These super-fancy glasses represent what it looks like to move through our lives using all 3 Eyes simultaneously. Pretty cool, right?

Bring the Two Minds into Alignment

Before jumping into implementing a change, there are a few tools that we've discussed thus far that will help us to make the most of our effort. The first is to put our subconscious and conscious minds to work for us. By now, we know that our subconscious minds are incredibly powerful and influential and that our best chance at creating a change is through aligning our conscious intentions with our subconscious minds. As we embark on any change, aligning the two minds is an important foundation.

John Bargh is a professor of psychology who studies human motivation. He says that often our self-improvement efforts fail because our conscious desires are not aligned with our subconscious motivations. New Year resolutions are a good example. Many of us start the year with the intention of losing weight, quitting drinking or beginning an exercise routine, for example, but find that even before January is over, the resolution has gone by the wayside. Bargh says this happens because while we consciously may want this change, our subconscious minds are not in agreement. We may have a conscious desire to go to the gym, for example, but we keep coming up with excuses for putting it off until tomorrow, and "tomorrow" just never seems to come.

Before starting on a COI, then, we should check in on our motivation. Bargh suggests that we ask ourselves a straightforward question: Am I truly committed to change? (2018). Only if the answer is 'yes,' should we proceed. If not, there may be some other change our subconscious minds feel drawn to addressing first, or perhaps there is a limiting belief that is undermining us that needs to be attended to. If we are not sure that our subconscious minds are onboard, or if our conscious *yes* is echoed by a subconscious *yes*, then we can apply one of the many tools we've discussed. The thought catching exercise, mindfulness techniques, or checking in with our bodies all can help us affirm alignment. Some additional clues to look for include making excuses, feeling consistently drawn to doing something other than what we set a goal to do, and finding it difficult to get started.

This happened to me when I started trying to write this book. I had the intention of writing it for more than a full year before I found the ability to focus and get it done. I'd have starts—I even had it as New Year's resolution and got a handful of pages and an outline done—but then something always got in the way. While I was passionate about the topic and felt compelled to write about it, whenever I had free time, something else felt more important to do first. I even built a whole chicken coup in my backyard to avoid writing!

Being aware that I was taking some pretty drastic steps to avoid writing, I talked to a coach and got clear on some of my subconscious thoughts and feelings that were getting in my way. These included a pretty big struggle with the imposter syndrome (who am I to write about this?) and not being clear about my intentions for the book. Once I got some more self-confidence and crystallized my goals for the book, my procrastination went away. I've since found the motivation to wake up at 4:30 am to write despite moving house (twice), working full time, and taking care of my family. While once writing was a battle, when the time was right, it became relatively effortless.

Bargh says the second impediment to creating change is the environmental cues that influence what we do. Other's behaviors are contagious, and our subconscious minds pick up on those cues to our benefit or to our detriment. If we want to make a change, we should surround ourselves with people and environmental cues that support the change and avoid the people and places that will undermine our goals. Are you a new teacher and want to improve your practice? Rather than hanging out and commiserating with your fellow new teachers (as comforting as that may be), try spending time with the teachers in your school who have the classrooms that you aspire to have. Observe their teaching, eat with them at lunch, read about inspiring educators. While you're doing all of these things, your subconscious mind is acclimating to this new way of being and will come on board to help you to create those same qualities in your classroom.

Want to make more money? Spend time around wealthy people. Have a drink at a fancy bar or hotel. When you spend time around people living the lifestyle you aspire to have, you are training your subconscious mind to accept that this is how you live, and it will start to help you get there. Want to lose weight? Avoid watching a lot of TV or being around people who have bad eating habits. Television shows are full of ads about eating unhealthy foods. Your friends who like to go to Happy Hour and eat bar food on Friday afternoon will detract from your goals.

Once our minds are in alignment and we're spending time in supportive environments, Bargh also recommends setting what he calls implementation intentions. Much like a theory of action, at the onset of initiating a change, we make a simple intention: When X happens, I will do Y. This intention is supported by a clear *where, when* and *how* to carry out that intention (2018). The key is to tie your intention with a highly likely event or situation that happens every day. For example, when I got in the right mental space to write this book, I set the intention: When I wake up first thing in the morning (X), I am going to write (Y). To get enough time, I set my *when* at 4:30 am daily, the *where* was my home. The *how* was to follow an outline for the book and to set incremental goals to complete each chapter.

Big Idea #19:

The foundation for any change initiative is to ensure that our conscious desires are aligned with our subconscious motivations.

Cycle of Inquiry

Now that our two minds are in agreement to change, the Cycle of Inquiry (COI) provides the process for putting it in place. A COI begins when we identify an area for improvement and the best way forward to improve in that area. Next, we implement the change and check in on the results. Based on the results, we revise our plan and implement it again. COIs have been used widely in education settings for decades, and they are a familiar way for many educators to map out a plan for change. They are also flexible; while they have a beginning and an end, the duration of a COI can range from a few weeks to a few months or longer. A big advantage of COIs is the tight progression between implementation, reviewing results, and refining the approach. We aren't stuck with something that isn't working for too long; if the change isn't producing the intended outcomes, it can be adapted. Finally, COIs align nicely with the 3 Eyes framework because there is a role for each lens to play in the process.

While there are various labels for each phase of a COI depending on the person or organization who has created it, the general cycle is the same. The COI we will be using here assumes a six-week timeframe and begins with a phase we call *Get Curious*.

Figure 5: 3 Eyes Cycle of Inquiry

Get Curious

In the chapter on Insight, we discussed how we should make curious self-reflection a part of our lives. "Curious" is the key word here. When we are curious, we're able to observe events from a learner's mind and remove some of the emotional charge that can get in the way of us seeing things clearly. If we approach self-work or school-work from a place of judgment, blame, or self-hatred, then we'll produce more of the same. At the very least, we'll block much of our progress. When we *Get Curious*, we do our best to approach ourselves, our colleagues and the challenges we hope to improve by remembering that we are all doing our very best.

When we *Get Curious*, we're gathering useful information to inform the area that we will focus upon during the rest of the cycle. For our self-work, this means capturing those habitual and disempowering thoughts that are preventing us from realizing our potential. Doing this can include activities such as the Thought-Feelings-Emotions log or applying one of the mindfulness activities, such as journaling. For school-work, this means understanding the context we want to change for the better. We become explorers in our own schools, districts, and communities and try to see them from a fresh perspective. The information we gather includes quantitative data on student achievement, attendance, and discipline. It also includes qualitative data acquired through site and classroom observations, feedback from family and community, and interviews with staff.

In this phase, we are choosing to see what needs to be attended to, and we get down to work collecting information. Depending on what we are seeking to address, this data collection could last a few days to a few weeks. Within the six-week cycle, we are using here, we will assume that the *Get Curious* phase lasts two to three days for self-work, one week for school-work. The primary lenses used during this phase are Intellect and Insight. With our Intellect, we marshal our cognitive resources to act as the observer and to collect quantitative data. Insight supports us to collect the qualitative data. For our self-work, we use our Insight to identify our thoughts and feelings and catalog them for analysis in the next phase. For our school-work, we use our Insight to understand the current context and to narrow in on places for further data collection.

Notice

Once we've got a solid source of data to review, the next step is to look at that data and to *Notice* what trends can be found there. The goal for this part of the process is to understand ourselves and our contexts more deeply so that we can identify the area we want to address.

For our self-work, we may want to ask ourselves questions such as:

- What are the persistent and regular thoughts I am having?
- What do I catch myself saying to others regularly?
- What are the strong emotions that I've been feeling and when?
- Have my thoughts been centered on a specific area of my life?
- What has gone really well over the past few days?
- How has my mood impacted my outlook?

For school-work, we are seeking to *Notice* trends that are coming up in our classrooms, schools or offices. Questions we might ask include:

- Which students do I regularly have negative (or positive) interactions with? Is there a commonality across these students?
- What are the trends in student achievement and behavior referrals in my school?
- What learnings from a past initiative can I apply to today's context?
- What part of my classroom is going really well?
- What are the common themes in the parent feedback we're collecting?
- How are our subgroups of students performing academically?
- What trends can we notice in our discipline referral data?
- Which groups of parents consistently show up for school events and which ones do not? And so on.

The questions we ask ourselves about the data should not be solely focused on our challenges, but instead, on understanding the context as deeply as possible. This comprehensive view requires that we put our attention on the whole picture, not just the parts that we want to improve. As we identify an area for change, we strive to do it from a place of love and compassion, and just see what common themes emerge without applying a lot of judgment or blame. By the end of the Notice phase, our goal is to identify 1-2 areas that we want to address during our COI.

During this phase, we will lean on all three lenses. We'll use our Intellect to analyze the data and identify themes. Our Insight helps us to recall lessons-learned from the past and to add greater depth of meaning and context to the data we are reviewing. Our Intuition supports us to identify the areas that feel like the right places to start. Caution: This is the part of the cycle where we can get stuck in our heads, analyzing and overanalyzing the data, unable to land on the right place to begin. Remember, this is a 6-week cycle. The worst thing that will happen is that we discover that we should have selected a different area to work on first. Even if this does happen, the lessons learned and the experiences we have had during the six weeks are still rich and worthwhile sources of insight. The process to identify the area of focus for a COI should take no more than two days in our six-week cycle, less if we are identifying an area for self-work alone.

Change the Story

Once we have identified an area for improvement and narrowed in on the specific part we want to improve over the next few weeks, then it is time to *Change the Story*. When we *Change the Story*, we develop a counter-story to the data that we are seeing. In other words, we're going to imagine what it would look like, feel like, and be like if it were different. We will also select the specific actions we will take to reach our new reality.

There is an approach to change management called *Appreciative Inquiry* that can be useful as we change the story. In Appreciative Inquiry, we take an assets-based point of view and look for the beauty in the areas we want to improve. Then, we seek to expand those places (Hammond, 2013). Just as with the Law of Attraction or self-directed neuroplasticity, Appreciative Inquiry encourages us to direct our attention towards what works about the way we approach our lives (for our self-work) or what is working in our organization (for our school-work). Sue Hammond is an expert in Appreciative Inquiry, and she says, "the tangible result of the inquiry process is a series of statements that describe where the organization wants to be, based on the high moments of where they have been. Because the statements are grounded in real experience and history, people know how to repeat their success" (Hammond, 2013, p. 1).

If using an Appreciative Inquiry approach for self-work, we consider goals we have accomplished, identify the specific actions we did to reach those goals, and apply those same techniques towards achieving our new goal. When I was setting out to write this book, for example, I recalled the last time I undertook a significant writing project: my dissertation. I brought many of the strategies I used in graduate school to support this effort— including the early morning writing sessions and use of a detailed outline. For school-work, this can include identifying an intervention that helped a group of students to improve and applying those strategies to a new group of students; recalling a successful policy implementation and recreating the steps taken to support this new effort; or a considering a positive interaction we had with a student that we usually have a hard time reaching, identifying what made that interaction different and doing it again.

During *Change the Story*, we'll write an affirmation that captures the new reality we want to create by the end of the six-week cycle. As we've discussed, affirmations are statements of fact and are stated in the present tense. Positive affirmations are healing and support positive self-esteem, while negative affirmations reinforce our fears, doubts, and self-criticisms. Since affirmations are messages we send to our subconscious minds to establish habitual ways of thinking and behaving, we want to be sure that our statements are aspirational and positive and are not stated in negative.

Using aspirations and positive visioning are also great examples of priming. As we discussed in chapter one, priming occurs when our subconscious minds pick up environmental cues that influence our unconscious associations. One of the examples we talked about was how we will replace the missing letter in S_O P with either an A or a U depending on whether our subconscious minds were primed with words or images associated with either cleaning or food. We can use the priming effect to our benefit by creating affirmations that make the change we seek more inevitable.

We can add some oomph to our affirmations by setting a measurable goal that we can work on during the coming weeks. When writing this book, I set the goal to write at least one hour a day and to complete one chapter every two weeks. I also hired a coach who kept me accountable. Even when I did not reach the chapter goal (which was most of the time), I did manage the hour-a-day goal most days, and usually was able to do even more than that. This kept me motivated and feeling like I was moving forward, even when my writing goals weren't met. Also, knowing that my coach was waiting for the content kept some positive pressure on me to keep going. I was writing for someone, not just myself, and I didn't want to let her down.

Since we want to get into the Act phase as quickly as possible, it is best to complete the *Change the Story* phase within a few hours for self-work and perhaps a day or so for school-work (if the change is being led by more than one person). The longer we stay in *Change the Story*, the more time we provide for our Intellect to step in to insert doubt and deliberation. While the Intellect part is important for identifying a measurable goal to focus upon, this is also when Insight and Intuition need to be employed to balance out our cognitive reasoning. In this phase, Insight helps us to draw upon lessons learned from the past and to identify the beliefs or parts of beliefs that we want to address. Intuition allows us to live-in to the new reality that we are seeking to create. It also helps us to develop an affirmation and felt experience of that new reality that will guide us in the coming weeks. When in doubt during this phase, we must allow Intuition to be our guide. When selecting an affirmation, we go with the theme that arrives first, and when seeking a course of action, we identify what feels like the right action, even if it doesn't logically make sense or we've never done it before. This is a six-week cycle, and we can change or adjust our approach before starting a new one, so we must try our best not to get stuck in Change the Story deliberating what to do.

Finally, as we start out on our self-work, it's important to remember that unpacking and transforming our beliefs is a lifelong process. We must try to resist the urge to address the big issues right away. We're peeling the layers of an onion, and this process stretches over the rest of our lifetimes. To get to the core of the onion, we address the outer layers first and trust that each new layer is peeled just as planned. Similarly, creating significant change in educational contexts can take years, so we should set goals for our COIs accordingly. If a school chooses to address student achievement, for example, they should identify what they want to accomplish in a year, and then what part of that goal can be accomplished in a six-week cycle and use that for the COI.

Act

Now the fun begins! Whether we have a daily mindfulness practice or not, when we Act, we try to live into our new way of being and to employ the strategies we identified when we changed the story. Whether doing self-work or school-work, I recommend that this include three things:

1. Taking a few minutes each day to state our affirmations and imagine the lived experience of the new reality.
2. Identifying at least one new mindfulness practice to begin or to strengthen.
3. Acknowledging the moments when we are experiencing our desired state throughout the day.

Since we've already discussed how to set affirmations, I won't add much more here, except that you have to say them! Affirmations are not like the *Set It and Forget It* rotisserie ovens that you see on the infomercials. Affirmations require daily positive attention so that they stay present in our minds, and mindfulness practices genuinely help. We all have busy lives, and some of us may not have time to do a 30-minute meditation practice or a daily affirmation session like SNL's Stuart Smalley. If we get creative, however, we can find a few minutes here or there to fit it in.

I am a single mom with a full-time job. Some examples of how I do it are to state my affirmation while I'm taking my shower, pausing for 30 seconds before entering a meeting to breathe and feel into my body, stopping to smell the roses while walking my dogs, and saying thank you in my mind before I eat. Also, I travel from school to school for work, so whenever I arrive even just five minutes early for a meeting, rather than checking my phone, I squeeze in a quick meditation session. Speaker and life coach Tony Robbins says that his personal transformation began in high school when he would repeat positive affirmations to himself over and over during his daily run. You get the idea. These mini-mindfulness moments will go a long way to supporting your transformation.

Since the goal is to focus on our desires, it's also powerful to stay as present as possible and to acknowledge when we are experiencing the state of being that we are seeking to create. For example, if our goal is to feel more joy and satisfaction at work, we acknowledge the moments when we feel that way— whether at work or not. When we start out, it could be that those feelings only come up we are in our garden, playing with our child or cooking dinner. While these moments are not happening at work, when we acknowledge them and give thanks, we are sending a message to the Universe that we want more of this good stuff to come. Through this practice, we train our bodies and minds to seek out more experiences of joy and satisfaction. The context is less important than the focus on the desired feeling, but if you can catch the feeling happening at work, great!

During the Act phase, all three 3 Eyes are at work. Our Intellect is busy attending to our goals and monitoring our progress. Our Insight is helping us to evaluate our state of being and bringing awareness to when limiting thoughts or beliefs may be derailing our efforts. Our Intuition keeps us in the present moment and mindful. Depending on how long it took to get through the first three phases, for a six-week COI, the Act phase will take between 4 or 5 weeks. It's plenty of time to try out a new practice, but not so long that we start to feel daunted at the amount of time we need to put in.

Celebrate Results

We did it! At the end of the six-week cycle, it is time to see how we did. As we have discussed throughout this book, this is a time to lean into curiosity and appreciation rather than judgment. Even if we haven't reached our goals, there were undoubtedly plenty of good things that happened along the way that we can lift up and celebrate. When we celebrate our results, we look for those good things and give ourselves hugs and high fives for trying. In this phase, we can be our own Believing Eyes, or we can check in with someone who can reflect our greatness back to us.

While we do a more in-depth celebration and analysis at the end of the full cycle, it's important to have a daily reflection as well. Taking just ten minutes at the end of the day to reflect on the high points and to recognize our accomplishments is a powerful practice. Firstly, it helps us to send signals to our minds and to the Universe that we want more positive feelings and experiences. Secondly, it keeps the forward momentum going.

During this phase, we use all 3 Eyes. We use our Intellect to identify our areas of growth and improvement. We use our Insight to check in on our thoughts and beliefs to see if we've nudged any limiting ones in a positive direction. We use our Intuition to ground into the gift of the present moment and to express gratitude for all that we've accomplished. Before we embark on the next cycle, then, we should take a day or two to rest, appreciate ourselves, and identify the strategies that really worked well for us. Don't skip this part—it's imperative!

Table five provides a summary of the steps.

Table 5: Sample Activities During a Cycle of Inquiry

Area of the Cycle	Notes and Examples
Get Curious: Gathering useful information to inform the area that we will focus upon during the rest of the cycle.	Duration: One week Examples: • Collect data for self-work:

	o Feelings, self-talk, physical sensations, things that we are preoccupied with during the day, etc. • Collect data for school-work: o Student achievement, parent participation, staff feedback, etc.
Notice: Making the unnoticed noticed so we can identify trends we want to address.	Duration: Up to two days Examples: • Self-work: o Common themes, thoughts, feelings that we want more of or that we want to change • School-work: o A group of students we want to support, a common complaint from parents, or a successful strategy we want to expand upon
Change the Story: Focusing on the new reality we want to experience, and identifying the affirmations and actions we will do to bring it into existence.	Duration: Up to one day Examples: • Self-work: o A concrete goal to achieve (such as losing a set number of pounds or writing an hour a day) and affirmations to support the effort. • School-work: o A concrete goal to achieve (such as improving reading scores for 5 specific students, or improving staff morale) and affirmations to support the effort.
Act: Putting our plans into action!	Duration: 4-5 weeks Examples: • Self-work:

	o Affirmations, visualization, mini-mindfulness moments, being the Believing Eyes for others, noticing on a daily (or even more frequent basis) when things are working in alignment with our goals and giving thanks, even if these moments are fleeting. o Enacting whatever changes in behavior we identified (such as meditating for 10 minutes, going on a run, or writing). • School-work: o Same as with self-work, but by enacting whatever work-based change we identified (such as targeted intervention for a group of students, initiating a new parent outreach effort, or implementing a new strategy to boost morale).
Celebrate Results: Celebrating what is working daily and at the end of the cycle.	Duration: 10 minutes daily during the COI, up to two days at the end of the cycle Examples for self-work and school-work: • End of day reflection or gratitude practice on what went well throughout the day. • Collecting evidence of student improvement. • When evaluating results, start by identifying what worked well, then consider whether the same conditions were in place for the things that didn't work as well. • Avoiding judgment or self-criticism if we didn't reach our goals; treating this moment an opportunity to set new goals for the next cycle.

> **Big Idea #20:**
>
> Cycles of Inquiry are a great way to marshal the discrete skills of each of the 3 Eyes into a focused process for creating the reality we seek.

A Few Final Thoughts

Throughout the book, we have likened the brain to a computer and discussed ways to rewire and customize that computer so that it functions the way we want it to. In our exploration of the brain, we learned of the profound impact that our earliest childhood experiences have on the way our subconscious minds develop. We also learned that our subconscious minds are in control almost all the time. This fact has implications for how we see ourselves, how we see others, and how we make meaning of our experiences. For anyone who interacts with children, this also means that we must be very intentional about the messages we convey to children about who they are and what they are capable of. Those messages have a lasting and potentially lifelong impact on our children's sense of self-efficacy and ability to realize their potential.

To begin to establish more control over our subconscious thoughts, and how we see our students and ourselves, we introduced two Theories of Action:

- **Self-Work:** If we use the 3 Eyes (Intellect, Insight, and Intuition) to see our lives and learned responses with more clarity and embark on a process to lovingly "rewire" the areas that do not align with who we want to be, then we experience greater self-appreciation and motivation to change. When we do that, we can realize our individual goals and engage with others to transform our educational settings.
- **School-Work:** If use the 3 Eyes to identify areas for needed improvement in our schools, and we create communities founded on trust and accountability, then we can use the power of teams to address the areas of needed change. When we do that, we can transform our educational settings into ones that support the adults and students alike to realize their potential.

Throughout the book, I have established the case that by intentionally using the information we gain through Intellect, Insight, and Intuition, we gain free will over the programming installed in our computers. To change the programming in ourselves, and by extension in the children we interact with, we must do self-work. This involves making friends with ourselves, developing a deep love and compassion for who we are and how we struggle, and then intentionally building a new way of being from the inside-out.

While self-work is crucial to our own sense of empowerment and self-realization, if we work in schools, it must be accompanied by school-work. This can range from addressing implicit bias to improving academic discourse to improving student attendance. The areas for improvement will be unique to every educational setting. When self-work and school-work are done simultaneously, we have the potential to create real transformations within our lives and in our students' lives.

At the root of all of this work is the invitation to love more. Love ourselves, love others, love our earth. Through love, we are able to tap into a deep appreciation for all that we already have and to see ourselves and others with more compassion and care. I truly believe the path towards a more equitable society is through increasing the amount of love we put into the world.

And the Path Continues...

So, where am I now? While through my self-work I have seen profound growth over the past three years, I'm not going to kid you—I've got a looooonng way to go! Through applying Intellect, Insight, and Intuition, I've peeled away a couple of significant layers of my onion--my sense of professional "victimhood" and the self-criticism that caused me to hold back who I really am. I am much more confident just being myself and letting the chips fall where they may. Even better, I'm really starting to like who I am, dirt and all!

But, as we've discussed throughout this book, the Warrior's path is a lifelong journey. Guess I who I found underneath those first two layers?! That little eight-year-old girl who refused to cry while watching E.T. Oh, snap! Yep, there she was, waiting to be brought to light! So, this is the layer I am working on now, and it's a toughie! Hiding my vulnerability is a core part of my self-identity. While I know that it needs to go, being strong and soldiering on has been one of the main ways that I have managed to cope all these years. It has helped me through some tough and painful times in my life and given me the sheer will to go on. For most of my life, I also counted it as among my greatest strengths and assets.

Through my self-work, however, I now realize that hiding my vulnerability has also caused me to feel alone, to isolate, and to refuse to ask for help. It's kept me from opening up to the deep love and connection that I yearn for. It's prevented me from truly releasing control and trusting the Universe. So, while I have valued and relied on this part of myself, it's got to go.

What am I doing now as I work on this layer? I'm taking bit by bit. First, I am trying to show myself an incredible amount of patience and compassion. Through mindfulness, I am learning to sense when I am putting on my armor, and instead, I am doing my best to feel the feelings that my armor shields me from. This means being okay with asking for help. This means allowing myself to completely fall apart after a devastating piece of news, letting the tears come and just being a puddle for a bit. This means moving past my own shame to admit that I am stressed out and tired and that I cannot keep up the armor anymore. This means facing the professional and personal risks that come with accepting that I can't do it all. This also means taking the risk to write this book and laying myself bare. It means choosing to step into the unknown of a new career path without the steps clearly marked before me.

I've come to see that true strength IS vulnerability. So, this is where I am, finally, making friends with those parts of myself that I started to shut off as a young child. Brene Brown has found through her research that, most commonly, it is middle-aged people who take on this work. She says that between our mid-thirties to early-sixties, many of us come to accept those parts of ourselves that we shut down as children and adolescents (2012). So, I guess that I am painfully typical and right on schedule, and I am so very grateful for it! It's nice to know that I am among friends, picking up the pieces of myself that I shed or sheltered for fear of not being safe, accepted or allowed.

For our education context, it is my sincere hope that we can prioritize supporting educators to develop a more profound love and appreciation for themselves. Through this deeper self-love, we will have a greater ability to join together as a community to transform our education system. Through compassion for ourselves and our peers, we can explore how our beliefs

Megan R. Sweet, Ed.D.

(especially our implicit biases) are affecting our ability to give our students the education they deserve. If we can swap out limiting beliefs and biases for those that are more expansive and loving, I genuinely believe that we can change the way that school is experienced by our students and families.

In a time where so many of our founding principles as a country and education system are coming under attack, my encouragement is to lean into love and hope and to set our sights on what our education system can be. Right now, it is the result of the institutionalized racism and oppression that has been a part of our country since it was founded. Rather than continuing to reflect and replicate those inequities, our education system can lead the transformation that our country so desperately needs. We have the power for our schools to be the places where these patterns break down and where we create a more equitable and empowering future for everyone, not just the powerful few. If we can let love for self and love of others lead the way, then we can have the self-confidence and the support of our communities to create profound personal and nationwide transformations. The Warrior's path through the use of the 3 Eyes can lead us there, and I hope you'll join me!

Appendix

Big Ideas from the Book

Big Idea #1	We have both subconscious and conscious minds that work together to shape our experiences and sense of self. Most of the time, it is our subconscious minds that are in control, reacting to stimuli based on past programming.
Big Idea #2	Our subconscious minds make associations and decisions based on our prior knowledge, often without our conscious awareness.
Big Idea #3	Our subconscious minds hold implicit biases that we may not consciously agree with but that nonetheless influence how we view and treat ourselves and others.
Big Idea #4	Educators must be supported to understand themselves (their backgrounds, biases, and beliefs), and to enter conversations with their peers about race, culture, and identity.
Big Idea #5	Successful change initiatives require ongoing and open communication, collaboration, and flexibility—both on the part of the policymaker and the stakeholders.
Big Idea #6	Educational change initiatives take time to be implemented, usually between three to five years. Speeding up the change process usually results in resistance and inconsistent implementation.

Big Idea #7	Individuals need to feel emotionally safe to fully contribute to a relationship, team or larger organizational culture.
Big Idea #8	Trust is a necessary component to all relationships, both personal and professional. We build trust through our character and our competence.
Big Idea #9	Love your employees through recognition, encouragement, and providing opportunities for personal and professional growth.
Big Idea #10	Collaborating with one's peers through PLCs is an effective and professionally rewarding way to create changes that will benefit students.
Big Idea #11	Perception, Cognition, Social Consensus, and Emotional Value affect how beliefs are formed and how closely with identify with them. The stronger our emotional response to a belief, the more deeply it is held in our minds.
Big Idea #12	Our values, beliefs, and social norms are subconscious filters that affect the way we experience the world. They are so well-established that we don't even know they are there. Like a pair of sunglasses, they color every aspect of how we experience our lives.
Big Idea #13	When our cultural norms (or schema) do not align with the circumstances we find ourselves in, it produces a reaction that our brains experience as a threat, which automatically shifts us into survival mode (fight, flight or freeze).
Big Idea #14	Our bodies are trying to communicate with us. Tapping into the sensations in our throats, chests or stomachs can give us valuable information about whether the thoughts we are having or actions we are considering taking are in our best interest.

Big Idea #15	Emotion plays a powerful role in our ability to access intuitive information. When we are in a happy and positive mood, we are better able to access our intuition. When we are in a bad or negative mood, we lose touch with our intuitive abilities.
Big Idea #16	To access our intuition, we must be in the present moment. Mindfulness supports us to be in the present and therefore aware of our thoughts, feelings and the subtle information that intuition provides.
Big Idea #17	What we focus our thoughts and feeling upon we bring to ourselves.
Big Idea #18	Through meditation, mindfulness, and intentionality, we can rewire the parts of our brains that have a negative influence on our thoughts and feelings.
Big Idea #19	The foundation for any change initiative is to ensure that our conscious desires are aligned with our subconscious motivations.
Big Idea #20	Cycles of Inquiry are a great way to marshal the discrete skills of each of the 3 Eyes into a focused process for creating the reality we seek.

Definition of Terms

Act: We try to live into our new way of being and employ whatever strategies we identified when we changed the story.

Affirmations: Statements of fact, stated in the present tense. Positive affirmations are healing and support positive self-esteem, while negative affirmations reinforce our fears, doubts, and self-criticisms. They are the messages we send to our subconscious minds, establishing habitual ways of thinking and behaving.

Belief: An acceptance that something is true or that something exists, even though the belief may be unproven or irrational.

Body Scan: Intentionally bringing the body and the mind together through mindful breaths.

Change the Story: We develop a counter-story, a counter-narrative to the data that we are seeing. We imagine what it would look like, feel like, be like if things were different.

Common Humanity: Seeing our experience as a part of the broader human experience and acknowledging that life is imperfect.

Compassion: Suffering with or relating to the pain of others.

Connection: The energy that exists between people when they feel seen, heard, and valued; when they can give and receive without judgment; and when they derive sustenance and strength from the relationship.

Conscious (mind): Self-awareness; the representation of who we perceive ourselves to be (our hopes, dreams, and individuality).

Context: Understanding the norms and values of the organization and of the stakeholders.

Culture of Power: Social norms and behaviors that advantage a group of individuals while simultaneously disadvantages those not in the empowered group. In the United States, white culture is advantaged over others.

Culturally Responsive Teaching: Including students' cultural references and norms in all aspects of instruction and classroom atmosphere.

Cycle of Inquiry (COI): Process by which we identify an area for improvement, determine the best way to improve that area, implement the change we have identified, check in on our results, and start again.

Decluttering: We remove the excess clutter (material objects) that surround us to create spaces that are organized and free of distraction.

Empathy: The ability to accurately assess other's viewpoints, which is achieved through fact-finding in three specific areas: time, context and point of view.

Emotional Freedom Techniques (EFT): Also known as "Tapping." EFT combines tapping acupressure points on the body while simultaneously stating phrases reflective of your current emotional state and replacing those statements with affirming ones.

Emotional Intelligence: The ability to recognize one's own emotions and those of others.

Emotional Regulation: Having a goal to either increase or decrease the duration and magnitude of an emotional response. Intrinsic emotional regulation comes from a person's self-motivated desire to control their emotional response, external emotional regulation is when one tries to control the emotions of another, interpersonal emotional regulation is attempting to control the emotional reactions between people.

Empathy: The ability to accurately assess others' viewpoints. In education policy implementation, it is achieved through fact-finding in three specific areas: Time, Context and Point of View.

Empowering Beliefs: Beliefs that allow us to realize our dreams.

Gratitude: Appreciating and valuing what already exists.

Grounding (or Earthing): Spending time in nature and touching the earth.

Implementation: Implementation is achieved when the people involved in creating change are able to plan for all of the small steps it will take to get from where they are at present, to where they eventually want to be.

Implementers: People who do the work to put a policy in place.

Implicit Bias: Attitudes or stereotypes that affect our understanding, actions, and decisions unconsciously.

Insight: Deep understanding of a person or thing. Insight is the practice of introspection, coupled with compassion and mindfulness.

Intellect: Logical thinking and reasoning, comprising primarily those left-brain functions that allow us to compute in math, to analyze problems and to form language

Intention: A purpose, aim, objective or goal.

Intuition: Knowing something based on instinct or feeling, rather than from conscious reasoning.

Journaling: The practice of writing down one's thoughts and feelings.

Law of Attraction: What you focus upon you bring to yourself.

Limiting Beliefs: Beliefs that hold us back.

Manifestation: The process by which something theoretical is made real. Manifestation occurs when something one feels and/or thinks becomes realized in some tangible way.

Meditation: The practice of making still one's mind and bringing attention back to the body and monitoring one's breath.

Microaggressions: Th everyday verbal, nonverbal, and environmental slights, snubs, or insults, whether intentional or unintentional, which communicate hostile, derogatory, or negative messages to target persons based solely upon their marginalized group membership.

Mind: The information that gets transmitted within our bodies, including our thoughts and the sensory information (sights, smells, tastes, physical sensations, and sounds) that help us to measure our level of safety and comfort.

Mindfulness: Being aware of our thoughts, feelings, body sensations, and environment in the moment; we are present with what is and not preoccupied with thoughts and feelings from past experiences or anticipating future experiences.

Mirror Work: The practice of looking deep into one's eyes and repeating affirmations.

Neural Pathways: The way information is communicated in the brain, which can be thought of as paths upon which information travels. Like a path on a hiking trail, the more a path is used, the deeper and more defined it becomes.

Neurons: Cells that communicate information from one neuron to another neuron or part of the body, sending information to our brains about our environment and physical state.

Neuroplasticity: The ability of the brain to grow and change in response to the way we use it. This means that we can intentionally change the physical structures of the brain based on the way that we think and focus our attention, and conversely, if parts of the brain are over- or under-developed, it can have influence our experience of thoughts and emotions.

Notice: Paying attention to trends (repetitive thoughts, issues, feelings) with the goal of understanding the problem deeply, so that we can more accurately identify the area we want to address.

Policy: A series of rules and procedures that are focused on a particular goal.

Policymaker: A leader (such as superintendent or principal) who initiates a change.

Point of View: Gathering input from diverse stakeholders and reviewing existing research on the potential policy.

Pride: A feeling of pleasure or satisfaction derived from one's own achievements.

Priming: When you become predisposed to something without the conscious decision to do so.

Programs: Learned responses to our environment that reside in our subconscious minds and that drive our responses (both conscious and unconscious)

Schema: A set of conceptual scripts that guide our comprehension of the world.

School-Work: The process by which we address the issues within our education settings that are preventing all students from learning at their full potential.

Self-Compassion: Treating oneself with patience, kindness, and understanding when one makes mistakes or is experiencing difficulties.

Self-Directed Neuroplasticity: When we use our minds to change the way our brain works so that we can change the mind for the better.

Self-Kindness: Treating oneself with care and providing comfort to oneself.

Self-Work: The process by which we come to know ourselves on a deeper level, identifying and changing the harmful and judgmental narratives that run in the back of our minds and that prevent us from living up to our potential.

Shame: The intensely painful feeling or experience of believing that we are flawed and therefore unworthy of love and belonging – something we've experienced, done, or failed to do makes us unworthy of connection.

Stakeholder: Anyone affected by a policy, including those who implement it.

Subconscious (mind): Powerful warehouse of information that holds our habits, controls our physical responses, and hard-wires learned responses to situations.

Time: Understanding the past history of the organization, present readiness to implement a policy, and the future vision of where the organization will be in five years.

Unconscious: Feelings, actions, or reactions that we are not aware of (such as a knee-jerk response).

Value: A person's principles or standards of behavior, and the regard given to something of worth; our values are often reflected in the way we live our lives.

Visualization: The pairing of imagination and emotion. When one visualizes an event, one tries to create that event in as much detail as possible, including sights, smells, textures, sounds, physical sensations, and emotions.

Brain Primer

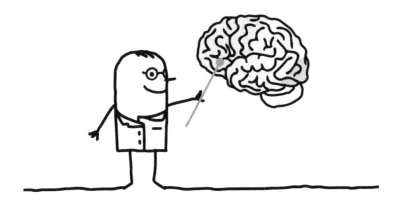

Okay, this actually extends beyond the brain! Our brain's reactions produce physical and emotional responses in the body and vice-versa. Here is a bit about how the parts work together and connect to the 3 Eyes.

Part of Brain or Body	Function	Connection to 3 Eyes Framework
Amygdala	The almond-shaped structure inside the limbic layer of the brain. Identifies and stores threats and negative emotions (anger, fear, anxiety).	Overactive amygdalas perceive threats everywhere, leading to persistent feelings of anxiety and fear.

	Designed to react instantly to perceived physical and social threats, and sends information directly to the Reptilian brain, releasing the stress hormone cortisol When cortisol is released, all other cognitive functions (such as learning, problem-solving and creative thinking) stop as the body prepares for fight or flight (Hammond, 2015, p. 40).	People can train their Amygdalas to be inhibited (or calmed) through psychotherapy or meditation focused on being safe (Hammond, 2015). EFT (Tapping) can also restore the mind to a state of calm and safety.
Autonomic Nervous System (ANS)	Controls physiological changes in our bodies based on our circumstances, primarily in response to whether or not we detect danger or safety. ANS has two branches: Sympathetic and Parasympathetic	In addition to the physiological functions related to fight/flight and rest/digest, our brains also respond to our environment. During the fight/flight response, our ability to learn and retain information is shut down so we can focus our attention on the necessary functions for survival.

	Sympathetic: Performs reactions related to fight or flight in our bodies, basically switching our bodies into the optimal condition for survival. This includes increasing heart and breathing rates (to send more oxygenated blood throughout the body, releasing glucose (for energy), dilating pupils (so we can see better), decreasing production of saliva (to slow digestion) and releasing adrenaline (for more energy). Parasympathetic: Rest and digest related to states of calm and does almost the exact opposite for the Sympathetic system, meaning that the pupils and salivary glands return to normal functions, breathing and heart rates decrease, we decrease glucose and	Zaretta Hammond's work has shown that students from marginalized communities are already on alert (their sympathetic nervous systems are triggered) based on past experiences in our society. Our job as educators is to build positive relationships with our students so that they feel safe and are able to learn at their full capacity (2015, p. 45).

	adrenaline amounts in the blood, and our digestion resumes/increases.	
Cortisol	Known as the stress hormone. Produced by the adrenal glands (that sit on top of the kidneys) and monitored by the hypothalamus and pituitary gland.	When we are in fight/flight/freeze mode, cortisol is running through our bodies. If we can tap into our physical sensations of stress, then we can employ a mindfulness technique so we can come back to a place of calm.
Hippocampus	Balances the fear and anxiety response of the Amygdala and plays a crucial role in memories—converting short-term memory into long-term memory. Holds short-term memory (lasting 5-20 seconds), working memory (lasting up to 20 minutes) and long-term memory. This is where active learning takes place, and where the	Uses emotions to establish long-term memory. EFT can help to regulate and reprogram the hippocampus to produce long-term changes to our learned responses.

	working memory seeks to connect new information to old (stored) knowledge (Hammond, 2015).	
Hypothalamus	Exists below the Thalamus. Tiny structure regulates several functions in our bodies, including the Autonomic Nervous System (ANS).	Triggers the release of hormones in our system. Fight or flight or rest and digest responses.
Insula	Located on the left and the right sides of the front of our brains. The insula is involved with our ability to do something called interoception, which means the ability to tune into the inner state of our bodies (such as whether we are hungry, thirsty, hot or cold) as well as tune into our deep feelings (Hanson, 2013).	Our ability to be insightful partially comes from this structure in our brains.
Limbic System (region)	Set of structures in the brain that primarily control emotion; contains	If the emotional response is strong enough, it will leave an imprint on the

	the Amygdala, Hippocampus, Hypothalamus, Thalamus, Septal Area and Cingulate Cortex Links emotions, behavior, and cognition together. Helps us learn from experience, manage our emotions, and remember. Records memories and experiences that produced positive or negative experiences in the past so that we can avoid the negative and maximize the positive in the future (Hammond, 2015).	brain in the form of a memory. Schema are a set of conceptual scripts that guide our comprehension of the world, and when our schema does not match the conditions we find ourselves in, it sends our brains and bodies into fight or flight mode. The stronger our emotional reaction is to a belief, the more likely we will be consciously aware of it. If a belief does not have a strong emotional change, we may not become consciously aware that it is there.
Neocortex Region	The newest part of the brain, 3-4 million years old. Slow in processing information, but really smart. It is where our executive function lives, which	Home of many of our conscious-mind activities and processing. Allows us to "act as an observer" of our thoughts and emotions and to

	is the command center of the brain. Controls planning, abstract thinking, organization, self-regulation, and imagination. Has the capacity to learn and to rewire itself.	choose a different reaction than our habitual response consciously.
Nervous System	Picks up information from our senses and our environment and sends them back to the brain for interpretation. The primary focus is to detect levels of safety and/or threat so that the body can act. Most of this process works through the Autonomic Nervous System (ANS).	Our ability to tap into our emotions and body sensations provide us a clue to what information is being communicated along our nervous system.
Neural Pathway	Avenues along which information travels in the brain. When the brain learns something new, it creates a neural pathway.	This is the key to rewiring our brains. We can teach ourselves to respond to stressors differently and to focus our attention on our goals—making them

| | The more we repeat the thinking/ processing of an activity, the more it gets stored into our brains in the form of long-term memories and automatic responses.

Neural Pathways form based on repetition— if we are no longer using a specific cognitive process or doing a specific physical activity, our brain reabsorbs those neurons, and we may need to "relearn" certain things due to lack of use. | more likely to be realized. |
|---|---|---|
| Neuron | Cells that communicates information from one neuron to another neuron across the structures of the brain or from other parts of the body.

Our brains contain tens of billions of neurons. | Recent research suggests we have neurons on our heart and gut regions and that these areas of our bodies are collecting and communicating information to our head-brains (Soosalu and Oka, 2012). |

	Our brains can grow more neurons through our continual process of learning (known as neuroplasticity).	
Neuroplasticity	Changes in synapses or neurons and the way they communicate information in the body. Our minds' ability to learn new information (thus creating new neurons) that can communicate with one another along neural pathways.	We can train our minds to react in a way that is different from our habitual responses. This is how we "rewire" our computers!
Prefrontal Cortex	The front part of the brain, behind our forehead, the part that distinguishes us as humans. Performs high order executive functions including forming language, solving math problems, and managing how we behave based on the social situation we are in.	Intellect!

Reticular Activating System (RAS)	Responsible for alertness and attention. The RAS scans our surroundings 24/7 for any significant changes to our environment or other relevant information connected to social status, physical survival, or strong emotions that might signal threat or reward. The RAS is particularly attuned to novelty (new information), relevance, and emotion (Hammond, 2015).	The RAS acts as a filter or fishnet, only allowing in things that reinforce thoughts and beliefs we already have, or alerting us to something new that may comprise a threat to our safety. The RAS is a significant cause of the "shading" of our lenses as it controls the very information that we take in and process.
Serotonin	A chemical and neurotransmitter in the human body that regulates mood, social behavior, appetite, sleep, and memory. This is the counter-chemical to Cortisol—we want more of it!	Some research suggests that soil contains a microbe similar to serotonin and a natural way to produce the effect of serotonin is through getting back in touch with the earth through Grounding.

Thalamus	The sensory relay station (sight, sound, taste, touch)— information travels from our nerves the RAS and then to the thalamus. The thalamus transmits this information to the cortex. The only sense not included is smell, which bypasses the thalamus and gets directly transmitted to the brain.	Monitoring our senses is important in regulating our emotional state. Mindfulness strategies such as body scans are a great way to touch back in with what our bodies are experiencing in the moment.
Vagus Nerve	Runs from the base of the brain down the spinal cord. This nerve controls many critical functions in the body, including the parasympathetic functions of the Autonomic Nervous System. The vagus nerve is a part of the "circuit that links the neck, heart, lungs, and abdomen to the brain" (Seymour, 2017).	Information from the heart and gut get communicated to the brain through this nerve. Supporting alignment between the heart, gut, and mind supports our happiness and well-being, as discussed in detail in the chapter on insight.

Works Cited

Armenta, C. & Lyubomirsky, S. (2017). "How gratitude motivates us to become better people," *Greater Good Magazine,* May 23, 2017. Retrieved from https://greatergood.berkeley.edu/article/item/how_gratitude_motivates_us_to_become_bette r_people.

Bargh, J. (2018). "How to use your unconscious mind to achieve your goals," *Greater Good Magazine,* January 30, 2018. Retrieved from https://greatergood.berkeley.edu/article/item/how_to_use_your_unconscious_mind_to_achieve_your_goals.

Berman, P. & McLaughlin, M.W. (1978). *Federal programs supporting educational change.* Implementing and sustaining innovations, 8. Santa Monica, Clif: Rand Corporation.

Bill and Melinda Gates Foundation (2017). *Outline of Our K-12 Strategy*: *November 2017.* Retrieved from http://k12education.gatesfoundation.org/index.php?pdf-file=1&filename=wp-content/uploads/2018/01/Outline-of-Our-K12-Strategy-11.17.17.pdf.

Boelman, L (2017). *Curiosity Invites Connection* [poem]. Used with permission from the author.

Booe, M (2018). "The importance of yoga for students," *Livestrong,* originally posted on January 30, 2018. Retrieved from https://www.livestrong.com/article/438314-importance-of-yoga-for-students/.

Breines, J. & Chan, S. (2012). "Self-compassion increases self-improvement motivation." *Personality and Social Psychology Bulletin.* 38(9) 1133–1143.

Brown, B. (2010). *The gifts of imperfection: Let go of who you think you're supposed to be and embrace who you are.* Hazelden Publishing, Center City, MN.

Brown, B. (2012). *The power of vulnerability: Teachings on authenticity, connection and courage* [Audio Recording]. Louisville, CO: Sounds True.

Brown, B. (2013). "Shame vs. guilt," *Brene Brown.* Originally posted on January 14, 2013. Retrieved from https://brenebrown.com/blog/2013/01/14/shame-v-guilt/.

Bryne, R. (2012). *The magic.* Atria Books, a division of Simon and Schuster, Inc, New York, New York.

Chemaly, S. (2016). Quoted by Staats, C., Capatosto, K., Wright, R., & Jackson, W. (Eds). "State of the science: Implicit bias review." *The Ohio State University: Kirwan Institute for the Study of Race and Ethnicity.* Retrieved from http://kirwaninstitute.osu.edu/wp-content/uploads/2016/07/implicit-bias-2016.pdf.

Chodron, P. (2001). *The places that scare you: A guide to fearlessness in difficult times.* Shambala publications. Boston, MA.

Chopra, D. (2018). "5 steps to setting powerful intentions." *The Chopra Center.* Retrieved from https://chopra.com/articles/5-steps-to-setting-powerful-intentions.

Choquette, S. (2018a). *"Creating your heart's desire guidebook: Principles for living the life you really want"* [electronic book]. Three Rivers Press, Nightingale-Conant Corporation, Illinois. Retrieved from https://members.soniachoquette.net/wp-content/uploads/course/creating_your_hearts_desire/Creating Your Hearts Desire Guidebook-sm.pdf.

Choquette, S. (2018b). *The pathway to joy* [electronic book]. Retrieved March 24, 2018 from https://soniachoquette.net/wp-content/uploads/2017/03/CHOQUETTE_PathwayToJoy_FINAL-1.pdf.

Church, D. (2013). "Clinical EFT as an evidence-based practice for the treatment of psychological and physiological conditions," Psychology 2013. Vol.4, No.8, 645-654. Published Online August 2013 in SciRes (http://www.scirp.org/journal/psych). Retrieved on March 30, 2018, from http://file.scirp.org/pdf/PSYCH_2013081215123494.pdf.

Church, D. (2017). "Comprehensive research analysis shows EFTs (Emotional Freedom Techniques) highly effective for PTSD," *Huffington Post*. Retrieved on February 26, 2018, from https://www.huffingtonpost.com/entry/comprehensive-research-analysis-shows-eft-emotional_us_58868d51e4b08f5134b623da.

Covey, S.M.R. (2006). *The speed of trust: The one thing that changes everything.* Free Press, a division of Simon and Schuster, Inc, New York, New York.

Davidson, C. (2017). Quoted in an article by Valerie Straus, "The surprising thing Google learned about its employees—and what it means for today's students." *The Washington Post*. Retrieved from https://www.washingtonpost.com/news/answer-sheet/wp/2017/12/20/the-surprising-thing-google-learned-about-its-employees-and-what-it-means-for-todays-students/?utm_term=.fcd1f6554136

Davidson, R. (2016). "The four keys to well-being," *Greater Good Science Center*. Retrieved on June 1, 2018 from https://greatergood.berkeley.edu/article/item/the_four_keys_to_well_being.

DeBrucke, Z. (2016). *Your inner GPS: Follow your internal guidance to optimal health, happiness and satisfaction.* New World Library, Novato, California.

Delpit, L. (1995). *Other people's children: Cultural conflict in the classroom.* New Press, New York, NY.

Delpit, L. (2012). *Multiplication is for white people: Raising expectations for other people's children*. New Press, New York, NY.

Delpit, L. (2018). "Lisa Delpit on power and pedagogy." *New Learning: Transformational Designs for Pedagogy and Assessment*. Retrieved on January 17, 2018, from http://newlearningonline.com/new-learning/chapter-8/lisa-delpit-on-power-and-pedagogy.

DeSteno, D. (2014). *The truth about trust: How it determines success in life, love, learning and more*. Penguin Random House, New York, New York.

DeSteno, D. (2018). "Three emotions that can help you succeed at your goals." *Greater Good Science Center*. Retrieved from https://greatergood.berkeley.edu/article/item/three_emotions_that_can_help_you_succeed_at_your_goals.

Dispenza, J. (2012). *Breaking the habit of being yourself: How to lose your mind and create a new one*. Hay House, Carlsbad, CA.

Doty, J. (2016). *Into the magic shop: A neurosurgeon's quest to discover the mysteries of the brain and the secrets of the heart*. James R. Doty, New York, NY.

Dufour, R. (2005). "What is a professional learning community?," *On common ground: The power of professional learning communities*. Solution Tree, Bloomington, Indiana, pp. 31-44.

Duhigg, C. (2016). "What Google learned from its quest to build the perfect team: New research reveals surprising truths about why some workgroups thrive and others falter," *The New York Times Magazine, The Work Issue, Reimagining the Office*. Retrieved on February 4, 2018, from https://www.nytimes.com/2016/02/28/magazine/what-google-learned-from-its-quest-to-build-the-perfect-team.html?smid=pl-share.

Emmons, R. (2010). "Why gratitude is good." *Greater Good Magazine*. Retrieved on March 30, 2018, from https://greatergood.berkeley.edu/article/item/why_gratitude_is_good.

Frederickson, B. (2003). "The value of positive emotions: The emerging science of positive psychology is coming to understand why it is good to feel good." *American Scientist*, Volume 91, pp 330-335.

Fullan, M. (2005). "Professional learning communities writ large," *On common ground: The power of professional learning communities*. Solution Tree, Bloomington, Indiana, pp. 209-223.

Fullan, M. (2008). *The six secrets of change: What the best leaders do to help their organizations survive and thrive*. John Wiley & Sons, Jossey-Bass, San Francisco, CA.

Google. (2017). Definition of intuition. Retrieved from https://www.google.com/search?sclient=psy-ab&safe=strict&biw=1024&bih=576&q=definition+of+intuition&oq=definition+of+intuition.

Google. (2017). Definition of insight. Retrieved on May 13, 2017, from https://www.google.com/search?q=definition+of+beliefs&oq=definition+of+beliefs&aqs=chrome..69i57j0l5.8012j0j8&sourceid=chrome&ie=UTF-8#q=definition+of+insight.

Google. (2018). Definition of neuroplasticity. Retrieved on May 31, 2018, from https://www.google.com/search?q=definition+of+neuroplasticity&rlz=1C1JPGB_enUS760US760&oq=definition+of+neuropla&aqs=chrome.1.69i57j0l5.8634j1j8&sourceid=chrome&ie=UTF-8.

Grant, B. (2018). "Antidepressant microbes in soil: How dirt makes you happy." *Gardening Know How*, Retrieved on March 30, 2018, from https://www.gardeningknowhow.com/garden-how-to/soil-fertilizers/antidepressant-microbes-soil.htm.

Hahn, T. N. (2017). *Happy teachers change the world*. Parallax Press, Berkeley, CA.

Hall, G. & Hord, S. (2006). Implementing change: Patterns, principles, and potholes. Boston: Allyn and Bacon.

Hammond, S. A. (2013). *The thin book of appreciative inquiry*. Thin Book Publishing Company, Bend, OR.

Hammond, Z. (2015). *Culturally responsive teaching and the brain: Promoting authentic engagement and rigor among culturally and linguistically diverse students*. Corwin, Thousand Oaks, CA.

Hanson, R. (2011). "Understanding neuroplasticity" [video]. *Greater Good Science Center*. Retrieved on May 30, 2018, from https://greatergood.berkeley.edu/video/item/understanding_neuroplasticity.

Hanson, R. (2013). "How to change your brain" [video]. *Greater Good Science Center*. Retrieved on June 1, 2018 from https://greatergood.berkeley.edu/video/item/how_to_change_your_brain.

Hawthorne, J. (2014). "Change your thoughts, change your world." *Jennifer Read Hawthorne: Words to Live By*. Retrieved on March 10, 2018, from http://www.jenniferhawthorne.com/articles/change_your_thoughts.html.

Hay, L. (2016). *Mirror work: 21 days to heal your life*. Hay House, Inc., Carlsbad, CA.

Heath, C. & Heath, D. (2010). *Switch: How to change things when change is hard*. Crown Publishing Group, a division of Random House, New York.

Jung, C. Quotation, accessed from the internet at, Brainy Quote on April 23, 2018, https://www.brainyquote.com/topics/intellect.

Kahneman, D (2011). *Thinking, fast and slow*. Farrar, Straus and Giroux, New York, NY.

Kalanithi, P (2016). *When breath becomes air*. Random House, New York, New York.

Ketelle, D. & Mesa, P (2006). "Empathetic understanding and school leadership preparation." *Kravis Leadership Institute, Leadership Review,*

Vol. 6, Fall 2006. pp. 144-154. http://citeseerx.ist.psu.edu/viewdoc/download?doi=10.1.1.578.2344&rep=rep1&type=pdf

Krech, G (2002). *Naikan: Gratitude, grace, and the Japanese art of self-reflection.* Stone bridge press, Berkeley, California.

Lencioni, P. (2018). *The five dysfunctions of a team* [graphic]. Retrieved on January 19, 2018, from http://www.executiveagenda.com/media/1278/fivedysfunctions.pdf

Levi, I. (1991). *The fixation of belief and its undoing: Changing beliefs through inquiry.* Cambridge University Press, New York, NY, 1991.

Lipsky, M. (1980). *Street-level bureaucracy: Dilemmas of the individual in public services.* New York: Russell Sage Foundation.

Lipton, B. (2008). *The biology of belief: Unleashing the power of consciousness, matter, and miracles.* Hay House, Inc., Carlsbad, CA.

Lipton, B. (2010). "Are you programmed at birth? How to transform the subconscious trance" [blog post].

Heal Your Life. Retrieved on October 19, 2018, at https://www.healyourlife.com/are-you-programmed-at-birth.

Lipton, B. (2012a). "Nature, nurture and human development" [blog post]. *Bruce Lipton.* Retrieved on October 2, 2016, at https://www.brucelipton.com/resource/article/nature-nurture-and-human-development.

Lipton, B. (2012b). "Mind, growth, and matter" [Interview transcript]. *Succeed Magazine.* Retrieved on January 15, 2018, from https://www.brucelipton.com/resource/interview/mind-growth-and-matter.

Lipton, B. (2013). *The honeymoon effect: The science of creating heaven on earth.* Mountain Love Productions, Hay House, Carlsbad, CA.

Lipton, B. (2014). "The spirit of a scientist: Interview of Bruce Lipton." Interview by Suma Varughes. *Life Positive Magazine*. Retrieved on October 2, 2016, from https://www.lifepositive.com/spirit-scientist/.

Livni, E. (2016). "The Japanese practice of 'forest bathing' is scientifically proven to improve your health." *Quartz*. Retrieved on March 30, 2018, from https://qz.com/804022/health-benefits-japanese-forest-bathing/

Love, N. (2002). *Using data/getting results: A practical guide for school improvement in mathematics and science.* Christopher-Gordon Publishers, Norwood, MA.

McLaughlin, M. (1991). "The Rand change agent study: ten years later." In A. R. Odden (Ed.), *Education policy implementation* (pp. 143-155). New York: State University of New York Press.

Merriam-Webster (2018), Definition of policy. Retrieved on January 23, 2018, from https://www.merriam-webster.com/dictionary/policy.

Mindful Schools (2017). "Evidence of the benefits of mindfulness in education." *Mindful Schools*. Retrieved on May 13, 2017, from http://www.mindfulschools.org/about-mindfulness/research/.

Moore, E., Michael, A. & Penick-Parks, M. (Eds.) (2018). *The guide for white women who teach black boys.* Corwin, Thousand Oaks, CA, 2018.

Neff, K. (2013). "Resilience and self-compassion" [lecture]. *Empathy and Compassion in Society*. Retrieved June 25, 2018, at https://www.youtube.com/watch?v=xyjLKgfV7Sk.

Newberg, A. (2006). *Why we believe what we believe: Uncovering our biological need for meaning, spirituality, and truth.* Free Press, a division of Simon and Schuster, Inc, New York, New York.

Obama, B. (2018). Quote about change, found in Good Reads. Retrieved on May 28, 2018, from https://www.goodreads.com/author/show/6356.Barack_Obama.

Ober, C., Chevalier, G., & Zucker, M. (2018). "Grounding the human body: The healing benefits of

earthing." *The Chopra Center*. Retrieved on March 30, 2018, from https://chopra.com/articles/grounding-the-human-body-the-healing-benefits-of-earthing

Odden, A. (1991). "The evolution of education policy implementation." In A.R. Odden (Ed.), *Education policy implementation* (pp. 1-12). New York: State University of New York Press.

Ortner, N. (2013). *The tapping solution: A revolutionary system for stress-free living*. Hay House, Inc., Carlsbad, CA.

Perez, T. (2007). *Sweetest I love you* [song.] Retrieved from https://www.youtube.com/watch?v=6_G9SEH_OV0.

Powell, J. (2015). "Opening the question of race to the question of belonging." Interview with Krista

Tippett on *On Being*. Original interview date, June 24, 2015. Retrieved on January 15, 2018, from https://onbeing.org/programs/john-a-powell-opening-the-question-of-race-to-the-question-of-belonging/

Pressman, J. & Wildavsky, A. (1979). "Implementation: How great expectations in Washington are dashed in Oakland; or, Why it's amazing that Federal programs work at all." California: University of California Press, Second Edition.

Psych-k (2018). *Conscious vs. subconscious*. Retrieved on January 15, 2018, from https://www.holistic-changes.com/conscious-vs-subconscious/.

reWork (2018a). "Unbiasing." *reWork*, a program of the Google corporation. Retrieved on February 4, 2018, from https://rework.withgoogle.com/subjects/unbiasing/.

reWork (2018b). "Watch unbiasing at work" [video]. *reWork*, a program of the Google corporation.

Retrieved on February 4, 2018, from https://rework.withgoogle.com/guides/unbiasing-raise-awareness/steps/watch-unconscious-bias-at-work/.

Safir, S. (2014). "Becoming a listening educator: The four traits of a listening educator are a willingness to slow down, genuine curiosity, attention to non-verbal cues, and self-awareness and empathy." *Edutopia*. Retrieved on March 17, 2018, from https://www.edutopia.org/blog/becoming-a-listening-educator-shane-safir.

Schmoker, M. (2005a). "Forward." *On common ground: The power of professional learning communities.*

Solution Tree, Bloomington, Indiana, pp. vii-x.

Schmoker, M. (2005b). "No turning back: The ironclad case for professional learning communities." *On common ground: The power of professional learning communities*. Solution Tree, Bloomington, Indiana, pp. 135-154.

School Planning and Management (2013). "Coloring the classroom." *School Planning and Management*. Retrieved on April 4, 2018, from https://webspm.com/Articles/2013/12/01/Coloring-the-Classroom.aspx?Page=1.

Senge, P., Scharmer, C., Jaworski, J., & Flowers, B. (2004). *Presence: An exploration of profound change in people, organizations, and society*. Doubleday, a division of Random House, Inc, New York, New York.

Seymour, T (2017). "Everything you need to know about the vagus nerve." *Medical News Today*. Retrieved from the internet on October 14, 2018, from https://www.medicalnewstoday.com/articles/318128.php.

Soosalu, G. & Oka, M. (2012). *mBraining: Using your multiple brains to do cool stuff*. mBIT International.

Srinivasan, M. (2014). *Teach breathe learn: Mindfulness in and out of the classroom*. Parallax Press, Berkeley, California.

Staats, C., Capatosto, K., Wright, R., & Jackson, W. (2016). "State of the science: Implicit bias review." *The Ohio State University: Kirwan Institute for the Study of Race and Ethnicity*. Retrieved from http://kirwaninstitute. osu.edu/wp-content/uploads/2016/07/implicit-bias-2016.pdf.

Staats, C., Capatosto, K., Tenney, L., & Mamo, S. (2017). "State of the science: Implicit bias review." *The Ohio State University: Kirwan Institute for the Study of Race and Ethnicity*. Downloaded from the internet on February 19, 2018. http://kirwaninstitute.osu.edu/wp-content/ uploads/2017/11/2017-SOTS-final-draft-02.pdf

Sue, D. (2010). "Microaggressions: More than just race." *Psychology Today*. Retrieved on August 7, 2018 from https://www.psychologytoday. com/us/blog/microaggressions-in-everyday-life/201011/ microaggressions-more-just-race.

Truebridge, S. (2014). *Resilience begins with beliefs: Building on student strengths for success in school*.

Teachers College Press, New York, NY.

Ullrich, M., & Lutgendorf, S. (2002). "Journaling about stressful events: Effects of cognitive processing and emotional expression." *The Society of Behavioral Medicine*, Volume 24, number 3, pgs 244-250.

United States Department of Education (2016). "The state of educator diversity in the educator workforce." *Policy and Program Studies Service Office of Planning, Evaluation and Policy Development, U.S. Department of Education*. Retrieved from http://www2.ed.gov/rschstat/eval/ highered/racial-diversity/state-racial-diversityworkforce.pdf.

Vanzant, I. (2015). *Trust: Mastering the four essential trusts*. SmileyBooks, Carlsbad, CA.

Wheatley, M. (2017). Quote found in, "How to improve communication skills." *Learner's Edge*. Retrieved on May 15, 2018, from http://www.learnersedgeinc.com/blog/how-to-improve-communication-skills.

Wheatley, M. (2018). "Warrior for the human spirit." *Margaret J. Wheatley*. Retrieved on February 9, 2018 from https://margaretwheatley.com/warriors-for-the-human-spirit-training-to-be-the-presence-of-insight-and-compassion/

Zhihui, F. (1996). "A review of research on teacher beliefs and practices." *Educational research*, 38:1, pgs. 47-65, DOI: 10.1080/0013188960380104. Retrieved from http://dx.doi.org/10.1080/0013188960380104.

Acknowledgments

Writing a book is a significant undertaking and one that requires the cooperation and support of countless people. To acknowledge all the people who supported me to write this book would make for another book altogether. These include the authors and researchers from whose work I have drawn inspiration, the life experiences that have shaped who I am and the countless teachers and students who have left me forever changed from their presence in my life. I'll narrow down my acknowledgments, then, to the people who directly supported me during the writing of this book.

First and foremost, great thanks go to my family. To my sweet, intuitive, and loving son Malcolm who has put up with an overly-tired mom and whose constant encouragement and support keep me going—always. You are my sun and moon and everything in between. To my parents, Bob and Sharifah Sweet, who raised and loved an independent kid and who are by my side always. I felt you with me in my early morning writing sessions. To my grandmother Ann Lovern, who continues to serve as the model of who I want to be when I grow up. To my sisters Anne Coronado and Karimah Sweet, who have shaped who I am in so many ways and who can make laugh harder than anyone else.

I also want to acknowledge my friends and colleagues. To Sara and Tom Stone and to Susan and Chris Andrien, who have taken me into your homes and encouraged me to keep going. Sara and Susan, you let me be myself, and that means the world to me! To Rachelle Rogers-Ard, whose friendship and patience grounds me and keeps me strong. Whenever I leave your office, I usually have a new book under my arm and always feel uplifted. To Alice Cheng, John Harris, and Myrna Alvarez whose friendship, Taco Tuesdays, and morning walks ground my son and me in a loving community. To Larry Cuban, my professor, friend, and mentor. You sharpen my mind and help me to be my best. To Delaine Eastin, my mentor, friend, and role model. Your fearless conviction and pioneering spirit have guided my career and helped me to find my voice. To Renato Almanzor. Our relationship continues to teach me so much about myself. Your counsel gives me the confidence to speak my truth and not shrink down. To my editor Rachel Neuburger. You were in my ear and literally on the page as I wrote. Your encouragement, humor, and great whit brought out my authentic voice and writing that I did not know I could produce.

Finally, to two of my oldest friends Sabrina Peters and Emiliana Simon-Thomas. We have come a long way from our No-Nukes club, but I still see glimmers of those little girls in the women we have become. While we can go long stretches without seeing each other, you each continue to inspire and ground me. Sabrina, your family has taken me and Malcolm in as a part of your extended family—we are honored to be amongst you. Your example as a woman, mother, and educator inspire me to be better every day. Emiliana, it's quite a privilege to be able to pop by and sit in your living room to talk brain science and mindfulness. Your humility, humor, and brilliance are so wonderful to see being played out on the global stage. I'm so glad that we met on the playground in first grade!

If I have failed to include your name here, please know that you are in my heart. I am grateful to all of the forces, seen and unseen, of the earth and other-worldly, that brought this work to life.

CPSIA information can be obtained
at www.ICGtesting.com
Printed in the USA
BVHW080954280119
538839BV00003B/256/P

9 781982 215279